THE BIBLE STORY
VOLUME I

—◆—

THE BOOK OF BEGINNINGS

(From Creation to Isaac)

the BIBLE story

The Book of Beginnings/Volume 1
Arthur S. Maxwell

Published jointly by

PACIFIC PRESS®
PUBLISHING ASSOCIATION
Nampa, ID 83653
Oshawa, Ontario, Canada

REVIEW AND HERALD
PUBLISHING ASSOCIATION
Washington, DC 20039-0555
Hagerstown, MD 21740

FOREWORD

The Bible is the most wonderful storybook ever written. It is full of stories, all the way from the first chapter of Genesis to the last chapter of Revelation.

These stories have been told over and over again for thousands of years, yet they are new and fresh and fascinating to every generation. They need to be retold today, so that the boys and girls of the twentieth century may see their beauty and catch their inspiration.

It is one of the strangest paradoxes of our time that just when the Bible is enjoying its widest circulation, millions of copies being sold every year, fewer people than ever seem to be reading it. Because in countless homes family worship and the reading of the Bible have been neglected, and parents themselves seldom open its pages, a whole generation is growing up with little or no knowledge of this wonderful Book.

Most modern children have heard little or nothing about the great Bible characters of ancient times, so familiar to their grandparents. Their heroes are not Daniel, Paul, and Peter, but Dick Tracy and Superman. They have never heard of the love of Jesus, and thus have been robbed of the greatest treasure their minds and hearts could possess. No wonder there is so much juvenile delinquency, youthful vandalism, and lawlessness.

In the author's opinion no greater contribution could be made to the welfare of society and the peace of the world than to lead children to love the Bible—to enjoy its stories, appreciate its teachings, adopt its standards, and find its God.

In writing *The Bible Story* the author has tried not only to tell the dear old stories in language that boys and girls of today can understand but also to reveal the golden thread which binds them—the love of God for the children of men, and His wondrous plan for their redemption.

The over-all purpose has been to provide what might be called a Bible for children by retelling all the old familiar stories in language that modern boys and girls can both understand and enjoy.

What fun it is to blow on the dandelion seed balls and see the soft furry particles fly away into the air. This is how the wind scatters the seeds of trees and of plants everywhere.

All of these retold stories are original. No paragraph or sentence has been borrowed from the work of any other author. In this sense it is an altogether new work, adapted to the needs and desires of the children of today.

Although an endeavor has been made to use only very simple words, such as the youngest child who is able to read can easily understand, these volumes are not intended to be readers for infants of preschool age. It is presumed that parents of these little ones will read the stories to them, explaining the longer words as may be necessary.

The Bible Story provides the widest coverage of any Bible storybook on the market. In its pages will be found all the stories suitable for telling to children, from Genesis to Revelation. In the telling of these stories the Bible narrative has been carefully adhered to without any addition of fanciful speculations.

Gladly the author confesses that in pursuing this undertaking he has caught a fresh glimpse of the wonder and the glory of the Book of books. Over and over again, whether it has been in the retelling of the story of creation and the Flood, the lives of patriarchs and prophets, the life and ministry of Jesus Christ, or the witness and martyrdom of the founders of the early church, he has seemed to hear, echoing down the centuries, those inexpressibly beautiful words, "God so loved the world."

Gratitude is due to the publishers, who with rare vision and enterprise have arranged for the illustration of these volumes with original paintings by some of the finest artists of our day, under the direction and inspiration of T. K. Martin, art director of the Review and Herald Publishing Association.

It is the hope **and** prayer of the author that, as a result of the publication of *The Bible Story*, thousands of children all over the world will be led to find new joy and interest in the Bible, and accept it for themselves, as indeed it is, the Word of the living God.

Arthur S. Maxwell.

Although Adam and Eve had been banished from Eden, they were blessed with children and given a beautiful home in which they laughed and sang and worshiped the Creator.

Dedicated to Boys and Girls in Every Land and to All Who Love the Bible

CONTENTS

PART I

Stories of Creation

(GENESIS 1:1-2:7)

STORY 1

Back to the Beginning

HAVE you ever wondered how everything in the world began? I suppose so. Most boys and girls do some time or other.

Those beautiful flowers in your garden, for instance—sweet peas, snapdragons, asters, hollyhocks, pansies—where did they come from?

"Seeds," you say.

True, but whence came the seeds?

From other flowers, of course, and those flowers from still other seeds, and so on back to—back to—well, back to where?

There's your dog. Where did he come from?

"We got him as a puppy," you say. "And he has a very fine pedigree."

So! That means you know his father's name, and maybe his grandfather's. But how about before that?

One thing you can be very sure of. Your dog's grandfather was once a puppy too, and he had a father, and a

13

← PAINTING BY HARRY ANDERSON   ©   BY REVIEW AND HERALD

This is a wonderful world, full of interesting things. How we should like to know how things began—the beautiful trees and flowers, the winding streams, and the happy birds.

grandfather, and so on back to—back to—well, back to when?

Then there's that rooster in your neighbor's yard that's crowing all the time. Where did he come from?

"An egg," you say.

Right. But a hen laid that egg, didn't she? To be sure she did. And she came from an egg herself not so long ago. And that egg was laid by another hen, and so on back to—well, back to what?

Then there's yourself. Where did you come from?

"Oh," you say, "mother brought me home from the hospital."

I suppose she did. But mother was a little baby once herself, wasn't she? And so was her mother, and her grandmother, and her great-grandmother, and so on back to—back to—well, back to whom?

Think of the mountains too and the wooded hills, the flowing rivers and the sand on the seashore—all the wonderful things of nature. Were they always here, just as you see them now? Or did they too have a beginning? And if so, when and how?

Many great men have tried to explain these things. And they have come up with all sorts of strange ideas and suggestions, most of them far from the truth.

There is only one place where you will find the true story, and that is in the Bible. If you will open this wonderful Book, you will find that the very first part is called Genesis, meaning the book of beginnings. Here you will find the answer to all your questions.

14

BACK TO THE BEGINNING

And that reminds me of a little girl I know. Once I asked her which chapter of the Bible she liked best. I thought she would say, "The twenty-third psalm"—the one that begins, "The Lord is my shepherd." But no. She said, "The first chapter of Matthew."

"I suppose you like it because it tells about how Jesus was born," I said.

"Oh, no," she said, "I like it best because it's all about the begats."

"The what?" I asked.

"The begats," she said.

So I opened my Bible and turned to Matthew 1. And there it was! "Abraham begat Isaac; and Isaac begat Jacob; and Jacob begat Judas," and so on.

I asked her if she knew what it meant, and she said, "No, but I do like the begats."

So I told her it meant that Abraham had a little boy, and Isaac had a little boy, and Jacob had a little boy, and so on, but I think she still liked the begats best.

Then I told her that, put the other way round, it would read, "And Jacob had a daddy, and Isaac had a daddy, and Abraham had a daddy," and so on.

She liked that better, but wondered how far back the story goes. I told her what Luke says about it.

In his third chapter, verse 34, Luke picks up the story at Abraham and carries it back farther and farther and farther. He tells us that Abraham was the son of Thara, "which was the son of Nachor, which was the son of Saruch," and so on.

15

Such strange names! But they were names of real boys in the long, long ago.

Then, having told us the names of Abraham's great-grandpa and great-great-grandpa, and so on, Luke says that Enos was the son of Seth, "which was the son of Adam, which" —how very, very wonderful!—"which was the son of God."

There the story ends. And it ends there because it cannot go any farther. It goes clear back to God and stops.

And that's where you go back to. And daddy. And mamma. And everybody's daddy and mamma. Everybody's grandpa and grandma. Everybody's great-grandpa and great-grandma. They all go back across the years, across the centuries, to God.

Not to a monkey, not to a tiny tadpole in the sea, but to the great and glorious God who made the world and man. And that's exactly what we read in the first words of the first chapter of the Bible, *"In the beginning God."*

STORY 2

How Everything Began

≈≈≈≈≈≈≈≈≈≈≈≈≈≈≈≈≈≈≈≈≈≈≈≈≈≈

MANY years ago I read a story about a boy who picked up a strange little object on the street. It was shaped like a horseshoe and had a mysterious name written on it. The boy tried to pronounce the name, but failed. He tried again and again. Then one day as he said the word a different way the object began to grow in his hand. It became bigger and bigger, until at last the horseshoe was as big as a **doorway**. He stepped through it and found himself in a foreign country, far across the sea.

Day by day, using his horseshoe, he visited all sorts of strange places. Then he thought he would like to see how people lived long ago. So as he whispered the magic word to the horseshoe, he said he would like to visit Rome in the days of the Caesars—and, presto, there he was!

Of course it was only a made-up story, but it does give us an idea. Would you like to go and see what the world was like back in the very beginning of time? You would? All right. Let's

imagine that there is an archway through which we can pass and travel back across the years.

Steady now. Careful. Now we are going through it. Everything around us is fading away. Chairs, table, carpet, radio set, are all disappearing. Faces are growing dim. Lights are going out. It is getting darker and darker.

Swiftly we speed back across the years. It's like being in a rocket plane. We streak over hundreds and thousands of years in a moment. Past the time when Jesus lived on earth. Past the

18

time of David. Past the time of Abraham. Past the time of Noah. Past the time of Adam.

Oh, dear, how dark it is! We can't see anything. All about us it is pitch black. Not a glimmer of light anywhere. Not the tiniest candle. Not the faintest star. Only darkness and night.

But we can hear something. It is the swishing, gurgling sound that water makes, just as we have heard it many a time at the seaside or when boating on a lake.

Water. And darkness.

19

As the Bible says, "Darkness was upon the face of the deep."

Of a sudden we realize we are not alone. Somebody is here. We know it. We feel it. Amid the darkness, the emptiness, the loneliness, God is here. The Spirit of God is moving "upon the face of the waters." God is looking upon the world He has created, planning what He will do with it.

Suddenly, from somewhere, we cannot tell where, we hear a voice. Musical, strong, resonant, unlike any voice we have heard before, it commands the darkness to give place to light.

Instantly the darkness vanishes. We can see again. Not very far. Only a few feet, a few yards perhaps, because all around us is a thick mist; but how wonderful is the light after the dark!

There is no blue sky; no bright sunshine, only a sort of brilliant fog, and under it water, water, everywhere. No land, just this vast, restless, heaving ocean. Not a man or a woman, not a boy or a girl, not a bird or an animal. No, not even a fish in the sea. Only light in the mist and on the water.

"And God saw the light, that it was good: and God divided the light from the darkness. And God called the light Day, and the darkness he called Night. And the evening and the morning were the first day."

The first day! The very beginning of everything in this old world. The beginning of time. The beginning of history. The beginning of all the happiness and sorrow of mankind. For it was on this day that the great and loving Creator, with a wonderful purpose in mind, drew near this blacked-out planet this dark little speck in space, and said, "Let there be light!"

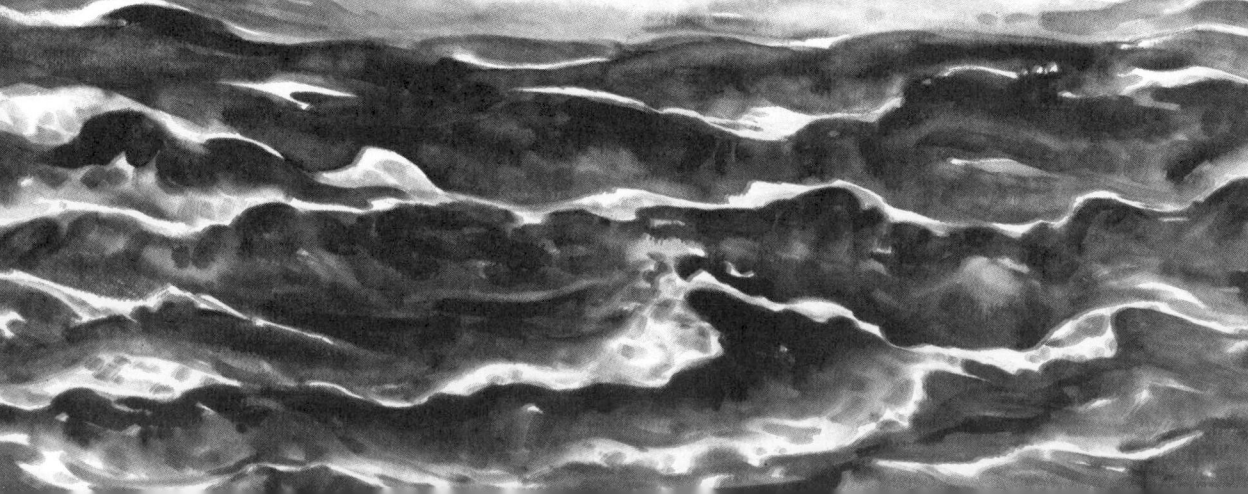

STORY 3

Great Preparations

AS THE light of earth's first day fades into night, something strange and wonderful begins to happen. Silently, mysteriously, the heavy, moisture-laden mist, that has held close to the ocean, begins to rise. All night and all the next morning it goes up, up, up, until it becomes a beautiful fleecy-white covering high above the world. Between it and the water below there is clear, fresh air, forming the "atmosphere," or the "firmament," as the Bible calls it.

"And God said, Let there be a firmament in the midst of the waters, and let it divide the waters from the waters. And God made the firmament, and divided the waters which were under the firmament from the waters which were above the firmament: and it was so. And God called the firmament Heaven. And the evening and the morning were the second day."

Perhaps you are wondering why God took one whole day of creation week to make something invisible like the atmos-

phere, when He gave one day to making the fish in the sea and another to making the animals. But things are not unimportant just because they cannot be seen. The fact is that what God did on the second day was of very great importance. Everything else depended on it.

You see, He was planning to make a beautiful world and fill it with living creatures, and they would all need air to breathe.

He planned to make birds too, and they would need air in which to fly. Without it they would be earthbound.

He was also about to make trees and plants and flowers, and He knew they would need nitrogen to help them grow. So He mixed it with oxygen and made air. Just the right amount of each. Not too much and not too little. Had He mixed in too little oxygen, all His creatures would have suffocated. Had

22

He mixed in too much, one spark would have set the world on fire.

God had yet another reason in making the air first. It was to divide the waters "above"—that is, in the clouds—from the waters "under"—or in the ocean. The air was to be a barrier between them. Without it raindrops from a mile-high cloud would have hit the earth like machine-gun bullets, and one heavy downpour would have just about destroyed everything.

How wise was it of God to make the atmosphere first—right after He had made light and before He made anything else! To have done otherwise would have been a dreadful mistake. His whole lovely plan might have been spoiled. But God does not make mistakes; and as we think of how He made the world we feel like saying with Paul, "O the depth of the riches both of the wisdom and knowledge of God! how unsearchable are his judgments, and his ways past finding out!"

And now earth's second day is ending. The beautiful white cloud is changing color. Shot through with gold, orange, red, purple, it slowly vanishes in darkness as night draws on.

Two days have gone, two out of six. And all that can be seen is the ocean, the great endless ocean. No land, no living creature, nothing but water. North, south, east, west, only water, water, water, the restless waves rolling on, on, on to nowhere.

In the darkness of the third evening it seems as though God has done nothing but lift the moisture-laden mist from the ocean. But He knows better. He is not impatient. He is not hurried. He knows that all is now ready for the next great step in creation.

Listen! He is speaking again: "And God said, Let the waters under the heaven be gathered together unto one place, and let the dry land appear."

Suddenly the great ocean begins to boil and seethe. There is a mighty shaking and shuddering as out of its depths rise the first needle points of land. Swiftly continents and islands take shape. Mountains and hills move upward as water drains from their sides in foaming cataracts.

What a night! What a day!

As morning dawns on the third day and light shines through the radiant cloud once more, it reveals no longer only an ocean, but great stretches of dry land. It is beautiful land, with lakes, rivers, and waterfalls, and beyond it all, the sea.

How very wonderful! Yesterday only an ocean. Today a beautiful world. Now we know for sure that God has a great plan in mind. He is building something, building a home for somebody He loves.

STORY 4

Birthday of a World

I T IS still early on the third day of creation week. There has been a very great earthquake. Land has mysteriously risen out of the ocean. Islands of all sizes and shapes have appeared. Majestic mountains, rolling hills, and lovely beaches are to be seen where before was only sea.

Yet there is something the matter. The land looks dark and barren save for bright, glittering patches here and there where precious metals lie on the surface. There is not a tree or a bush or a blade of grass anywhere. Surely God does not intend that anyone shall live in a place like this?

Wait a minute. It is too soon to judge.

Listen! God is speaking once more. The same wonderful voice which said, "Let there be light," now commands, "Let the earth bring forth grass, the herb yielding seed, and the fruit tree yielding fruit after his kind, whose seed is in itself, upon the earth."

Now look. What a transformation! Look at those hills! They are barren no more. They have turned a vivid green.

25

From one side to the other they are covered with grass, bushes, trees. Look at the mountains! See those glorious pines, cedars, redwoods, reaching clear to the top of the highest peaks.

And the fields. What beauty! Look at all the flowers! Masses of them, of all kinds and colors. They look like a living carpet laid over the whole countryside. Buttercups and daisies, poppies and marigolds, bluebells and daffodils, hollyhocks and snapdragons, geraniums and delphiniums, orchids and begonias, roses and lilacs. How did God think of so many? And how marvelously He made them all, each with its own delicate design, its own special coloring and fragrance!

"And the earth brought forth grass, and herb yielding seed after his kind, and the tree yielding fruit, whose seed was in itself, after his kind: and God saw that it was good."

It must have been very, very good, with God as the designer and maker of it all, and He so pleased with it. The Bible says that all things were created for His "pleasure," and I like to think that He enjoyed Himself making all these plants and flowers and trees, each one different from all others—and then giving to all the power to reproduce, each "after his kind," through all time to come.

God seems to have been specially interested in the trees "yielding fruit," or, as we would say, the fruit trees. With what care He made the apple trees, the plum trees, the pear trees, the orange trees, the lemon trees, the avocado trees, and all the rest, each with its own choice fruit! And I think I can see Him moving from one beautiful tree to another, perhaps even tasting the fruit, and saying to Himself, "He'll like this. I'm sure he will. And this, and this."

For God was not thinking of Himself but of someone else. Someone who at the moment existed only in His mind, but who soon would be a real, living being. Someone to whom He was planning to give all this beauty and loveliness, all this wealth of treasure and delight.

All the gold, silver, and precious stones that sparkled and glittered amid the grass and the flowers; all the bountiful provision of nuts, fruits, and grains; all the glory of this wonderful new world—all was for *him,* to make him happy, to cause him to turn with loving adoration and thankfulness to his Creator.

The world was nearly ready for him. Nearly, but not quite. There were a few more things to be done.

"And the evening and the morning were the third day."

STORY 5

The First Rays of Sunshine

IN THREE short days the dark, water-covered globe has been changed into a Paradise of beauty.

Driven up from the ocean depths by some mighty, unseen force, land has appeared. Just as wonderfully, and with equal suddenness, the new continents and islands have been covered with grass and flowers, shrubs and trees, of every shape and size and color.

Now the fourth day has come. Evening and night have passed. Dawn is breaking. From the bright cloud above the "firmament," or atmosphere, a gentle light makes God's work of yesterday seem more beautiful than ever.

But look! Something is happening. Up there. In the cloud. It is breaking up. See! Beyond it is a bright light, a ball of fire. What can it be? It is the sun! Already its first warm rays are sweeping over the lovely landscape, making it more and more like one gorgeous fairyland. Flowers are turning eagerly toward the shining orb as ferns lift their fronds and trees their branches in joyous welcome.

29

What a beautiful world God made, when He created the green fields of grass, the lovely ponds, the graceful trees, the pretty flowers, and everything that was pleasant to the eyes.

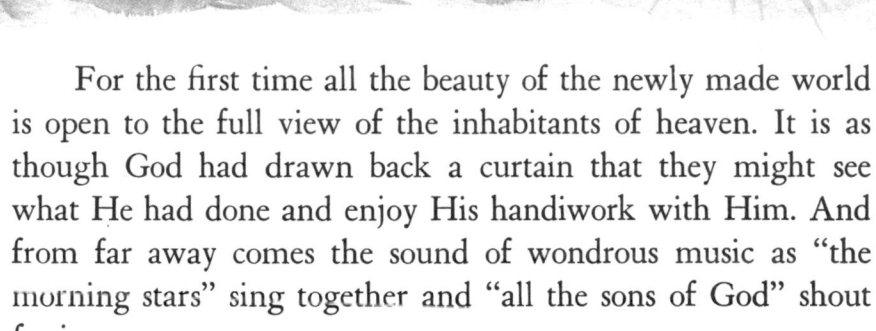

For the first time all the beauty of the newly made world is open to the full view of the inhabitants of heaven. It is as though God had drawn back a curtain that they might see what He had done and enjoy His handiwork with Him. And from far away comes the sound of wondrous music as "the morning stars" sing together and "all the sons of God" shout for joy.

Around the sun is a circle of blue, getting larger and larger as the cloud dissolves away. It is the sky, the lovely blue sky, which, reflected in the lakes and seas below, makes them the same color as itself.

Yonder is the moon, pale and dull as yet, waiting for nightfall, and the setting of the sun, to take its place as the light of the world.

"And God said, Let there be lights in the firmament of the heaven to divide the day from the night; and let them be for signs, and for seasons, and for days, and years: and let them be for lights in the firmament of the heaven to give light upon the earth: and it was so. And God made two great lights; the greater light to rule the day, and the lesser light to rule the night: he made the stars also.

THE FIRST RAYS OF SUNSHINE

"And God set them in the firmament of the heaven to give light upon the earth, and to rule over the day and over the night, and to divide the light from the darkness: and God saw that it was good."

And it *was* good, very good, and very necessary; for without the light and warmth of the sun many of the plants and trees that God had made could not have lasted very long. He knew this and in His wisdom made provision for the care of all. He knew too that the animals He was about to make would love the sunshine and that they could never keep healthy and strong without it. Man would love it too and need it just as much; and for his sake, most of all, those first rays shone upon the earth.

In all this God was thinking not only of today and tomorrow but of many days to come. The world He was making was not to be just a toy, a plaything, which He would toss away when He was tired of it. He was building for eternity. That is why He planned that the sun and the moon should mark the passing not only of days but also of the "seasons" and the "years," many seasons and many years. If the man He was about to make should choose to love and obey Him, he could enjoy this gloryland for ever and ever.

And though man was not yet made, I feel sure that there lurked within the heart of God the hope that all his years would be happy years, time without end; that the sun might never mark a day of sorrow nor the moon a night of pain.

"And the evening and the morning were the fourth day."

STORY 6

Out of the Silence—A Song

BEAUTIFUL beyond words was the world that God had made, but with all its beauty it was a silent and an empty world.

As morning dawned on the fifth day there was not a sound to be heard anywhere save the sighing of the wind in the trees and the gentle splashing of waves upon the beaches. No lion roared, no elephant trumpeted in the forest glades, not even one little frog croaked in the fern-covered pools. Not a dog barked, not a coyote howled, not a crow cawed. Nor was there any sound of human voice. No shout of a boy, no laughter of a little girl. How quiet it must have been!

But God did not want an empty world or a silent world. He was making it to be inhabited. All His great preparations of the first day, the second day, the third day, the fourth day, were to make ready a home for a multitude of living creatures.

So now, as the sun shines warm and bright upon the lovely flower-covered countryside and the deep-blue sea beyond, God moves into action again.

32

"And God said, Let the waters bring forth abundantly the moving creature that hath life, and fowl that may fly above the earth in the open firmament of heaven.

"And God created great whales, and every living creature that moveth, which the waters brought forth abundantly, after their kind, and every winged fowl after his kind: and God saw that it was good.

"And God blessed them, saying, Be fruitful, and multiply, and fill the waters in the seas, and let fowl multiply in the earth."

What a day that was! What a wonderful day! Don't you wish you really could have been there? I do. I would have loved to see God make the first goldfish, the first silver salmon, and send the first great whale surging through the sea like a giant submarine.

I am sure He enjoyed Himself making all those fish. But how did He think of so many different kinds? The big, fat porpoise and the little brown trout, the marvelous blue sailfish and the tiny little minnow, the sunfish and the starfish, the swordfish and the cuttlefish, the crabs and the shrimps, the lobsters and the eels. I cannot begin to think of them all. But God thought of them all. He designed them and made them, all in one day,

all different, all with the power to live and move and breathe—under water! How wonderful is our Creator! How we should honor Him and adore Him!

But making a thousand varieties of fish all at once was not enough. On this selfsame day He made the birds also. His marvelous mind planning the wingspread of the eagle, the gorgeous plumage of the peacock, the gay colors of the parrot, the mimicking skill of the mockingbird, and the radar outfit of the bat.

Look! Just look at them! What a marvelous sight! Hundreds and thousands of birds of every size and shape and hue rising from the earth, flapping their wings, swooping up and down, hither and yon, in the first full joy of living!

And what is that? Hark! The silence is broken at last. From everywhere comes the sound of singing. The birds are singing! The air is filled with their lovely songs.

From far up in the blue comes the sweet lilt of a skylark; from deep in the forest the lovely song of a nightingale and the gay trill of a canary. Near by, sparrows are twittering, doves are cooing, and cuckoos, meadow larks, killdeers and whippoorwills give forth their merry songs in praise to Him who made them. What wonderful harmony!

"And the evening and the morning were the fifth day."

34

STORY 7

The Animals Appear

FOR a few short hours the birds had the world all to themselves. They flew happily through the air, perched on the branches of the trees, and walked, or waddled, through the flower-strewn meadows. No doubt they thought—if birds can think—what a lovely place God had made for them.

But God had not made all this marvelous wonderland just for them. Early on the morning of the sixth day a loud roar came from some forest glade. Birds in nearby trees soared into the air, chirping and twittering. Then, curious to see what it was all about, they flew back; and, lo, there was a great golden yellow creature with a fine, strong face, a long, hairy mane, and a bearing like a king. It was the very first lion to roam the earth.

But look over there! Whatever can that be? Such a strange animal, with four long legs, a big, long neck, and such a funny face! A giraffe, of course! Ambling by with its head high in the air, it almost knocks the smallest birds out of the trees.

And what is this? A huge creature with legs like tree trunks, big flapping ears, little tiny eyes, and on the end of its nose a

sort of long tube, which it tosses this way and that, sometimes even putting it into its curious little mouth. Oh, dear! What fun God must have had making the elephant!

Here come a couple of horses, perhaps black, or brown. Such graceful creatures they are, as they canter by with their heads tossing and their feet going clippety-clop, clippety-clop, in perfect rhythm.

Now a couple of zebras, with strange markings on their coats; two leopards, with spots all over them; a crocodile, waddling on its little short legs; a hippopotamus, lumbering by with its huge mouth open; a camel, with its humps; a deer, with its antlers; a bear, with its long, shaggy coat.

What a procession! And to think that God designed and made them all in such a little while! Yet this is not half the story. Not only did He make all the big animals; He made the tiny ones too.

Just look there! A little dog, barking and scampering about as all dogs have done from that day to this; a cat, walking by with stately steps; a monkey, swinging from branch to branch; a chipmunk, making funny faces; a gopher, burrowing fast to hide itself in the earth; a chameleon, changing color every few seconds; a squirrel, with a big, bushy tail, scurrying around looking for something to bury. And all these created in a single day! It is too wonderful for us to understand. Just think! Every one of these marvelous creatures was not only made *alive* but

made to see, hear, smell, taste, and eat, just like you and me. More than that, each one was given the power to reproduce, to make baby animals just like itself.

You can draw animals on paper; you can make animals of clay or Plasticine; but you can't make one of your animals live. You can't make them walk or run or eat, can you? No, indeed. And just as well, for if you could, what would mother do with them all about the house? And how would she feed so many?

No, we cannot make animals that live. We cannot make even a toad or a mosquito. But God can. And God did. In His creative mind every animal, every insect, had its beginning, and at the sound of His voice they sprang forth from the earth to do His bidding.

"And God said, Let the earth bring forth the living creature after his kind, cattle, and creeping thing, and beast of the earth after his kind: and it was so. And God made the beast of the earth after his kind, and cattle after their kind, and every thing that creepeth upon the earth after his kind: and God saw that it was good."

God was pleased with His work. "It was good," and He was happy. His creatures were happy too, and peaceful. Yet creation was not complete. Something was missing. The most important thing of all remained to be done. And God had left it till the last.

STORY 8

God Makes Man

≋≋≋≋≋≋≋≋≋≋≋≋≋≋

HAVE you ever planned a wonderful surprise for mother? For her birthday, perhaps? I am sure you have. You may have bought something for her from a store or made it all by yourself. A cake, maybe, or some candy, a painting, or a piece of needlework. Whatever it was, I know you could hardly wait for the day to come when you could give it to her. What excitement you felt as the moment drew near!

Something like this thrill must have been in the heart of God on that sixth day of creation week. For that day was going to be a birthday too, and He knew it.

All that week He had been getting the present ready. Such a present! A whole world! A beautiful, beautiful world. A world full of treasures—gold, silver, and precious stones; a world full of food—nuts and fruits and grains and pure, sparkling water; a world full of loveliness—trees and ferns and flowers; a world full of marvelous living creatures—birds, fish, and animals of every kind and color, creatures to study, to play with, to laugh at. What a wonderful present for somebody!

39

Before God made man He had everything ready for his happiness. A beautiful garden was prepared for him to live in. Then with loving care He created him in His own image.

Yes, and all the time God was preparing this present He was thinking of this somebody, and saying to Himself, "I hope he will enjoy it; I hope it will make him happy. I hope he will notice all the things I have done to please him, and that he will love Me in return."

At last, when everything was ready, and God had done everything He could think of to make the world a Paradise, He said:

"Let us make man in our image, after our likeness: and let them have dominion over the fish of the sea, and over the fowl of the air, and over the cattle, and over all the earth, and over every creeping thing that creepeth upon the earth.

"So God created man in his own image, in the image of God created he him; male and female created he them."

"In his own image!" Like God! How very, very wonderful!

God might have said, "Let us make man like a monkey." But He did not. He might have said, "Let us make man like a lion, only bigger and stronger." But He did not. He might have said, "Let us make man like an eagle and give him wings to fly over the highest mountains." But He did not. Instead He chose to make man like Himself. He could have given him no greater honor, shown him no greater love.

"And the Lord God formed man of the dust of the ground."

When God made the animals and birds, "he spake, and it was done." They came leaping, springing, out of the earth at the sound of His voice. But with man it was different. God "formed" him. With infinite wisdom, infinite patience, infinite

40

tenderness, He molded the noble head, the kind face, the strong body. And He built into him something more wonderful than television—the power to see; something more wonderful than radio—the power to hear; something more wonderful than radar— the power to think and talk and remember. Best of all, God made it possible for him to love and laugh and worship.

Finally the task was completed, as with infinite gentleness God gave the last finishing touches to His masterpiece. There upon the earth from which he had been made lay man—the very first man—silent and still like some beautiful statue, awaiting the gift of life.

And God "breathed into his nostrils the breath of life; and man became a living soul."

How near God must have come to him! So very, very close! The mouth of God touching the mouth of man! Perhaps, who knows, God kissed him. Perhaps, too, there were tears of love in His eyes as He bent low over this wonderful creature He had made, so like Himself, so dear to His heart.

Suddenly, as God whispered to him, gently, tenderly, lovingly, breathing into him His own wonderful life, Adam awoke and looked up into the face of his Maker.

STORY 9

Adam's First Meal

LEAPING to his feet, Adam looked around him for the first time at the beautiful world in which he found himself. I wonder what he thought? And what he said?

Of course there was nobody for him to talk to except himself—and the animals. That some of them were nearby goes without saying, for animals are always so full of curiosity, aren't they? I can almost see a little dog licking his hand and a cat brushing past his leg, hoping to be noticed, and maybe a horse nosing in to be petted.

Coming from all directions are other animals, perhaps a lion and an elephant, a bear and a beaver, a big fat panda and a saucy little chipmunk—all so friendly, but gazing wide-eyed at the magnificent creature before them. Somehow they seem to recognize in him their leader and master; and as he strides forth over the soft, green grass, they follow him gladly, leaping and frisking about in pride and joy.

Happy cries of welcome fill the meadows and forests as the grand procession moves on its way over hill and dale, by shady

43

← PAINTING BY HARRY ANDERSON   ©   BY REVIEW AND HERALD

How happy Adam must have been to have all the animals love to come to him. It must have been fun to name them all, for he knew just what to call them when he saw them.

pool, tinkling stream, and sandy lake shore. As Adam pauses to marvel at some fresh wonder of creation, perhaps some tall, graceful tree or radiantly beautiful flower, more animals appear from the forest glades, while birds swoop low to see what is going on. Instinct tells them that this tall, handsome being, with the flashing eye and kingly bearing, has been given "dominion over the fish of the sea, and over the fowl of the air, and over every living thing that moveth upon the earth."

There is no fear in any heart. Adam is not afraid of the tiger that follows close at his heels, nor the tiger of him. A deer plays with a leopard without thought of harm, and antelopes, buffaloes, camels, dromedaries, and kangaroos graze together in perfect peace and harmony.

Seeing the animals eat reminds Adam that he is hungry. But what is there for him? His eye turns to some purple grapes hanging from a vine, then to some bright red berries, and again to clusters of nuts on the trees. Could these be his food? As he wonders which he should take he hears the voice of God saying to him, "Behold, I have given you every herb bearing seed, which is upon the face of all the earth, and every tree, in the which is the fruit of a tree yielding seed; to you it shall be for meat."

So he may take his choice. They are all for him. But with so many lovely things before him he finds it hard to decide which to eat first. A banana, perhaps, or an apple, or maybe some almonds, or pecans, or a bunch of grapes? Dear, oh, dear, what a problem!

Just which he took first we shall never know, but of one

thing we may be certain—Adam's first meal must have been the finest man ever ate—with every item on the menu fresh from the Creator's hand, brought into existence but three short days before. How tasty, how luscious, it must have been! Don't you wish you could have shared it with him?

And did it ever occur to you how wonderful it is that God created the grass before He made the animals to eat it? And that He made fruit trees and nut trees before He made man, who would need these things for food? And that when He created trees and vines and grasses God made them so that they could draw from the earth just those very elements—minerals and vitamins—which living creatures need to keep them alive? How carefully, how marvelously, did He plan every detail of this glorious new world of His!

It is now late in the afternoon of the sixth day. Already the sun is sinking toward the western horizon. God's work of creation is almost over. Everything he intended to do to make a perfect home for man has been done. Everything, that is, save one. He has created the earth out of nothing. He has divided the land from the sea. He has covered the mountains and the hills with gorgeous trees and flowers. He has made the birds, the fishes, and the animals. Crowning all, He has made man "in his own image"—man, His masterpiece, the supreme object of His love, for whom all this beauty and abundance has been provided. Yet there is one thing more that remains to be done —one last beautiful blessing to bestow, the sweetest, loveliest act of all creation week.

STORY 10

Fairest Creature of Creation

A S ADAM watched the animals basking in the warm sunshine, or playing happily in the meadows, he soon noticed that they were in pairs. Every animal had a mate. Alongside the majestic lion strode a sleek and slender lioness. Behind the antlered stag moved a graceful doe. With the powerful bull was a gentle cow. Near the tiger was a tigress. Close by the bear was a she-bear. Not far from Mr. Rabbit was Mrs. Rabbit, and so it was with the giraffes and the zebras, the rhinos and the antelopes, the opossums and the squirrels.

Only Adam was alone. Truly the animals were as friendly to him as they could be. When he called to them they stopped and looked at him with their great, big, wondering eyes, but they couldn't say a single word in return. The little dog seemed to understand him best, and it was clear that he wanted to speak ever so badly, but all he could do was wiggle and jump about and bark and wag his tail.

Many times Adam must have wondered why there was no mate for him. Perhaps he began to search for one. Perhaps, out

47

← PAINTING BY RUSSELL HARLAN   ©   BY REVIEW AND HERALD

Like a great master artist, God put the finishing touch on creation by making a woman, the world's first mother, the most lovely of all His creatures, whom Adam named Eve.

of the ache in his heart, he called and called, hoping that someone like himself might hear his voice and answer. Perhaps he
half expected to see some beautiful creature come gliding through
the forest toward him to be his special friend and companion.
But no one came.

As he lay upon the grass thinking of these things his sense
of loneliness increased. The earth was very beautiful, the animals *so* friendly and amusing; but there was nobody for him to
talk to, nobody with whom he could share his thoughts, nobody,
that is, save God.

Suddenly Adam began to feel very sleepy. This was strange,
he thought. He had never felt like this before. What could be
happening to him? He tried to keep awake, but it was no use.
Moment by moment he became sleepier and sleepier, until at
last he could keep his eyes open no longer. The earth, the flowers,
the trees, the animals—all faded away and were forgotten as he
fell into deep slumber.

Now God drew near to him again, as near as He had been
a little while before when He had breathed into his nostrils the
breath of life. With one swift touch of His gentle, creative hands
He removed a rib from the sleeping form before Him, closing
up the wound with infinite skill.

"And the rib, which the Lord God had taken from man,
made he a woman."

What a strange thing for God to do! If He could make
the sun, the moon, and the stars by saying, "Let there be lights
in the firmament of the heaven"; if He could make all the animals by saying, "Let the earth bring forth the living creature

48

after his kind," why did He not say, "Let there be a woman"? And why, after making Adam the most marvelous creature in His wonderful new world, did He take a rib from his perfect body to make his life companion?

There must have been a good reason why God acted thus, and I like to think it was because He wanted Adam to know that his wife was truly part of him, so that he would ever treat her as he would himself. The Bible tells us that God made Eve to be "an help meet for him," from which our word "helpmate" has come. And what a lovely thought that is! She was to stand by his side always, helping him, working with him, planning with him, and sharing life's joys with him.

But let us watch God at work again. Of Adam's rib we are told He "builded" a woman. Even as He had "formed" man of the dust of the ground, so now, with infinite wisdom and skill, He fashioned the one who was to become the mother of the whole human race. How perfectly He molded the features of her lovely face! How gracefully He arranged her long, flowing hair! With what loving thought He placed within her mind and heart all the tenderness, all the gentleness, all the sweetness, all the endless store of love He wanted every mother to have!

In less time than it takes to tell there stood before Him the fairest creature of all creation, her eyes sparkling with the joy of life, a tender smile giving her pretty face a beauty beyond compare.

And now, slowly and gracefully, she takes her first few steps as God brings her "unto the man."

Wonderingly she looks down at the sleeping figure before her. Who can this be?

Dreaming perhaps of the companion he hopes to meet someday, somewhere, in this wonderful world God has given him, Adam stirs and opens his eyes. Oh, wonder of wonders! There before him stands someone more beautiful than he had dared to hope for, a being so choice, so noble, so altogether lovely that he can scarcely believe that she is real. Looking into her bright, kindly, understanding eyes, he knows at once that this is his mate, the dear companion for whom he has been longing.

"And Adam said, This is now bone of my bones, and flesh of my flesh: she shall be called Woman, because she was taken out of Man."

It is love at first sight. Instantly both seem to know that they belong to each other. Eagerly they link hands and walk away together. As king and queen of the glorious new earth they wander through the flower-filled fields, over the tree-studded hills, down by the wave-swept shore, exploring the wonders of God's creation and marveling at the glory of His power.

Meanwhile, not far away, silently watching over them in tender love, and smiling at their perfect happiness, is God Himself, His joy complete in theirs.

PART II

Stories of Eden and the Fall

(Genesis 2:8-5:27)

STORY 1

Man's Garden Home

SOMEWHERE amid all the wonder and beauty of the world which He had created "the Lord God planted a garden eastward in Eden; and there he put the man whom he had formed."

Have you ever planted a garden? Exciting, isn't it? Especially in the springtime when you sow seeds and wait for the little green shoots to come up. And how thrilling it is when the flowers begin to bloom, the corn ripens, and the cabbages and heads of lettuce get fat and hard and ready to eat!

But when God planted the Garden of Eden it was different. He did not need to plant seeds. As Creator He could make full-grown trees and bushes appear immediately, all in the right place, just where He wanted them. He could say, I want a cluster of tall cedars here and a grove of silver birches there, and they appeared at His word. He could call for a hill to be covered with pines, another with redwoods, and another with oaks, and it was so. He could call for a valley to be carpeted

53

Adam and Eve loved each other and everything God had given them. They were happy tending this beautiful garden so full of delightful vines, fruit trees, and fragrant flowers.

with yellow buttercups, another with scarlet anemones, and another with sweet-smelling hyacinths, and it was so.

How glorious, then, must have been the garden home that He planted specially for His beloved Adam and Eve! We can only imagine its splendor as we think of some of nature's wonderlands that we know and love today.

Notice that God did not build them a palace, though He had made them king and queen of the world; He did not erect some fine stone house for them, with marble floors and electric light, though He had given them silver and gold in abundance. Instead He made them a home amid the trees and flowers.

For walls this home had palms and firs and maples, and its floor was the soft, sweet-smelling earth, gorgeously carpeted with bluebells, marigolds, and primroses. For roof it had the spreading branches of trees and, beyond, the glorious dome of heaven, where the sun gave light by day and the moon and the stars by night.

There was no need for shelter, for in that far-off day when the world was born there was neither rain nor storm. Instead "there went up a mist from the earth, and watered the whole face of the ground."

In man's first home there was no bedroom as we think of bedrooms, only cozy, moss-covered nooks among the bushes, or flower-strewn couches beside tinkling streams. Its parlor was a hillside overlooking some entrancing bay or sandy, lakeside cove. Its music room was among the trees, where the birds trilled

their lovely songs. Its kitchen and larder were the fruit-laden vines and bushes ever loaded with good things to eat.

Surely no home ever built by man has been so beautiful, so peaceful, so altogether perfect, as this glorious garden home which the Lord God planted in Eden in the long ago.

How happy Adam and Eve must have been as, hand in hand, they hastened from one lovely scene to another! I can almost hear Eve crying out, "O Adam, look at this pretty flower. And this, and this! And smell their fragrance! What a wonderful place to live!"

Walking eagerly along, they come suddenly upon two remarkable trees, different from all the others they have seen, and both loaded with brilliantly colored fruit. As they stand admiring this new and wonderful sight, God draws near to tell them that they are now in the very center of their garden home; that one of these trees is "the tree of life" and the other "the tree of the knowledge of good and evil."

"And the Lord God commanded the man, saying, Of every tree of the garden thou mayest freely eat: but of the tree of the knowledge of good and evil, thou shalt not eat of it: for in the day that thou eatest thereof thou shalt surely die."

Die? they wonder. What does God mean? And why has He planted a tree in the garden of which we mustn't eat?

Still wondering, they go on their happy way together as the sun sinks lower and lower toward the horizon.

What a day it has been! With its dawn the animals came

leaping out of the earth at the call of their Creator. Then He made man, in His own image, after His likeness. At last, crowning all, with infinite wisdom, love, and understanding, He fashioned His most beautiful and perfect work, a woman.

And now this wonderful day is drawing to a close. Shadows are lengthening, birds are twittering in the trees, and strange sounds from the forest tell that the animals know by instinct that night is near.

Gazing westward at the blazing glory of the sunset, Adam and Eve stand awe-struck as the sky is filled with wondrous colors and a new beauty glows from every tree and flower.

What can be happening? they wonder. Is their beautiful world coming to an end so soon? But God whispers to them, "This is but the sunset; watch for the glory of the dawn."

"And God saw every thing that he had made, and, behold, it was very good." It was. Very, very good. The earth, the sea, the trees, the flowers, the animals—all as perfect as God could make them—and now this happy pair of human beings, so stately, so beautiful, so sweetly innocent, bowing in reverent worship of their Maker. What more could even He desire?

Creation is complete. God's work is done. His purpose of love is fulfilled. No wonder heaven rings with His praise as once more the stars sing together and all the sons of God shout for joy.

STORY 2

A Day to Remember

S THE sun went down on the sixth day of creation week a wondrous calm fell upon all the countryside.

Gradually the twittering of the birds and the grunting of the beasts in the forest grew fainter and fainter until at last there was a great silence as the stars came out and all nature was bathed in brilliant moonlight.

Somewhere in the garden, perhaps in some lovely mossy glade, sat Adam and Eve, marveling at the beauty of the evening as they had at the glory of the day.

Suddenly, out of the silence, came a voice—tender, kind, and musical—and they knew at once that it was the voice of God. Then it was that God told them—for He *must* have told them, otherwise how could they have known?—that this new day, their first day upon the earth, was to be a holy day. He must have told them too how He had created everything about them in six days and that now, on the seventh day, He and they would rest together.

57

The Bible says that "on the seventh day God ended his work which he had made; and he rested on the seventh day from all his work which he had made. And God blessed the seventh day, and sanctified it: because that in it he had rested from all his work which God created and made."

God did not rest because He was tired, for God does not get tired. Rather He rested because His work of creation was finished. The world was as perfect as He could make it. There was nothing more He could do to it to serve the purpose He had in mind.

He rested also because He wanted to set Adam and Eve an example for them and their children to follow. You see, God not only "rested" on this day, He "blessed" it and "sanctified" it. This tells us clearly that He was thinking not of Himself but of His earthly children.

He blessed the Sabbath that it might be a blessing to *them*. He "sanctified" it—set it apart as a holy day—not for Himself, but for *them*. And how true it is, even today, six thousand years later, that all who keep the seventh day holy find a blessing in it that others never know! In some wonderful way the peace and happiness of heaven come into their hearts as they follow the plan God gave to Adam and Eve in the beginning.

And now once more we see them on that quiet evening in the long ago as they listen reverently to the voice of their Creator and learn that their very first day upon the earth is to be a holy day, spent together with Him.

They are perfectly happy, and in the morning as the rising sun wakens them from their first night's sleep, God

leads them forth through the beautiful garden He has made to be their home. Perhaps He reveals to them some of the marvelous secrets of creation. As they stop to admire some beautiful tree or lovely flowering shrub, He explains how they draw their food from the soil, how the sap rises through the trunk and so out into the branches, the twigs, the leaves, the flowers.

Perhaps He tells them how a beautiful white lily grows from a little brown bulb, how a little blue-speckled egg becomes a yellow canary, how a tiny seed inside a rosy apple grows to be another apple tree.

Maybe He explains how a bee gathers honey, how a spider spins its web, and how white milk comes from a red cow that eats green grass. Perhaps, too, He reveals the secret of flight— how an eagle can fly above the mountains and a hummingbird hover like a helicopter.

We shall never know exactly what they talked about that day, but it must have been thrilling to walk through creation with the Creator. Many a time, as Adam and Eve gasped in wonderment at the beauty and perfection of everything around them, they may well have exclaimed, "Great and marvelous are thy works, Lord God Almighty!"

Certainly it must have been a very, very happy day indeed, that first day of rest and worship and communion with God. Adam and Eve remembered it and talked about it all their lives.

And God wants every Sabbath to be as nearly like that first Sabbath as possible. That is why, when He gave the Ten Commandments on Sinai, He said, "Remember the sabbath day, to

59

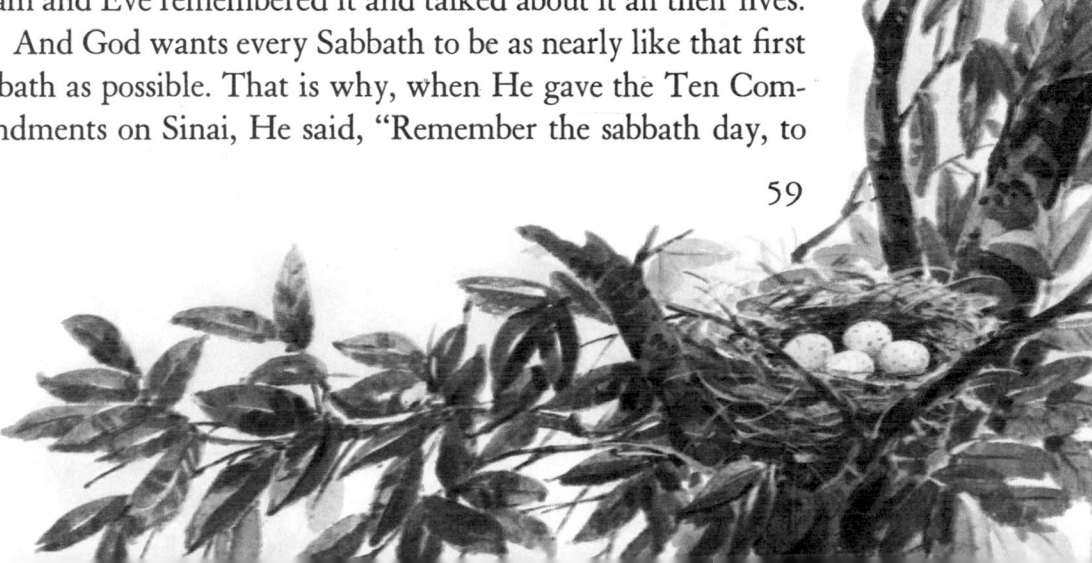

keep it holy. Six days shalt thou labour, and do all thy work: but the seventh day is the sabbath of the Lord thy God." He added, so we wouldn't forget, "For in six days the Lord made heaven and earth, the sea, and all that in them is, and rested the seventh day: wherefore the Lord blessed the sabbath day, and hallowed it."

Thousands of years after that first Sabbath in the Garden of Eden, God was still thinking about it. He could not forget it, and never will. And because it was so happy, so beautiful, so truly blessed, He wants everybody else to remember it too. For every Sabbath can be like that one, if we want it to be, just as happy, just as beautiful, just as blessed. All we have to do each seventh day is to remember to keep it holy, to walk and talk with God, and to worship Him as the Creator of the heavens and the earth.

STORY 3

The First Mistake

THOSE first few days that Adam and Eve spent in the Garden of Eden must have been supremely happy ones. They didn't have a care in the world. Not a single one.

How well they felt! How strong, how radiantly healthy! They didn't know what sickness meant. They never had a headache or a toothache. Day after day they awoke from untroubled sleep fresh as daisies, ready for anything.

Life was one glorious picnic. Their work was so pleasant and easy it was just like play, for all that God asked them to do in their lovely garden home was "to dress it and to keep it." There were no weeds, or thorns, or thistles, to bother them. Nor did they have to spend long hours putting up buildings or making clothes. The climate was so warm and delightful that they didn't need any.

As for food, the finest fruits, nuts, and vegetables, full of life-giving vitamins, were all around them. They could have all they wanted, just for the picking. So they didn't have to do any cooking or washing up!

61

Such was man's first home, beautiful, peaceful, and happy beyond words. And Adam and Eve might be living there still if they hadn't made one sad mistake.

That mistake, which seemed so small and unimportant at the moment, proved to be the turning point in their lives. Afterward nothing was ever the same again.

It happened this way: One day Eve went for a walk by herself in the garden. She wanted to take another look at the two wonderful trees in the center of it, with all their beautiful, brightly colored fruit.

Why, she wondered, had God given one of them such a peculiar name—"the tree of the knowledge of good and evil"? What was "good"? What was "evil"? And why mustn't she eat its fruit? How could it possibly do her harm?

It seemed strange that God, after giving so much, should

62

not give all. Why should He hold back one tree? But Eve had no thought of disobeying Him, not then. No doubt she told herself that He would explain all about it someday. There was probably some good reason.

As she turned away, perhaps to look again at the lovely "tree of life," she was startled to hear someone speaking to her.

Who could it be? The only voices she had heard up to now had been the voice of God and the voice of Adam. Now someone else was speaking. Astonished, she looked this way and that, but saw nobody. Then she noticed that the voice was coming from a serpent.

How very remarkable! An animal that could talk! She waited to see if it would speak again.

It did; and its voice was so friendly and pleasing that any fears she may have had disappeared. After all, it was rather

63

nice to have someone else to talk to, even though it was only a serpent.

Who was this serpent? And why was it able to talk?

The Bible tells us that it was "the Devil, and Satan, which deceiveth the whole world." First known as Lucifer, the light bearer, he was once a leader of the angels in heaven; but he rebelled against God, and was cast out of heaven. Then it was that he came to this earth to take revenge on God by trying to spoil His plans for man's happiness.

Of course, Eve did not know all this, not then. If she had, she surely would not have listened to him. All she knew was that here was a most unusual creature talking to her in a kindly, gracious voice.

And the serpent said, "Yea, hath God said, Ye shall not eat of every tree of the garden?"

"Yes," replied Eve innocently. "That's right. 'We may eat of the fruit of the trees of the garden: but of the fruit of the tree which is in the midst of the garden, God hath said, Ye shall not eat of it, neither shall ye touch it, lest ye die.'"

"Ye shall not surely die," said the serpent in a joking sort of way, as though nothing of the sort could possibly happen.

Strange! Eve must have thought. This creature is actually contradicting God! How dare he? It isn't right.

She should have run from the scene and told Adam and God what had happened. But she didn't. She stayed. She listened. And here she made her first mistake.

And, oh, what a lot of sorrow came from it! What a price there is to pay for dallying with evil!

≋≋≋≋≋≋≋≋≋

STORY 4

The Test of Love

≋≋≋≋≋≋≋≋≋≋≋≋≋≋≋≋≋≋≋≋≋≋≋

AS EVE stood there by the tree "of the knowledge of good and evil," listening to the soft-spoken words of the serpent, the first doubt entered her mind.

God had said that if she ate of this tree, she would die. Now the serpent said she wouldn't die. Who was right? Could it be that God had not told the truth?

As she thought this over, the serpent followed with another evil thought. Said he, "For God doth know that in the day ye eat thereof, then your eyes shall be opened, and ye shall be as gods, knowing good and evil."

Thus he suggested that God had been unfair to her and Adam, that He was holding back something that belonged to them. There was a sly hint too that God was jealous of them, afraid that they might become as wise as Himself.

It was very wicked and mean of the serpent to say such things when God had been so good to Adam and Eve. But Satan is like that. He is always working against God, always suggesting

5

unkind and hateful things, always trying to make trouble and separate friends.

That suggestion of his about "knowing good and evil" aroused Eve's curiosity. Up to that moment she had not known anything about evil. She may even have asked herself what Satan meant by the word. What was evil like? Then she thought it might be nice to find out.

That is always dangerous. It is the first step along the path to trouble and sorrow. We need to be ever on guard against suggestions to try some wrong thing to learn how it feels, or how it tastes. We should not seek to know evil. We are far better off without such knowledge. No one has to put his hand into a bucket of tar to know it's black.

Little by little Eve surrendered to Satan's tricks. First she began to doubt God's word. Then it seemed as though it wouldn't matter much if she disobeyed Him. Then she was ready to touch the forbidden fruit.

Finally the temptation was more than she could stand. She reached out her hand, took of the fruit, and ate it. The taste was delightful. She wondered why she had hesitated so long. Surely the serpent must be right after all. God couldn't possibly have meant to keep her from eating fruit as lovely as this.

She gathered more and took it to Adam, explaining to him what had happened, "and he did eat."

No doubt he said to her, "But I thought God told us not to eat this fruit." And she probably said, "Oh, it's quite all right. The serpent told me I wouldn't die, and, you see, nothing has happened to me. Maybe God made a mistake."

But God had not made a mistake. He had had a good reason for telling Adam and Eve not to eat of that tree. It was His way of finding out if they really loved Him. He had given them so much—every good thing He could think of—and He yearned for their love in return. Did they really love Him? Would they love Him always? How could He be sure?

There is one never-failing test of love, and that is obedience. If we truly love father and mother, we will gladly obey them.

So it was that God told Adam and Eve not to eat of that tree. It was a simple test. If they had loved Him sincerely, with all their hearts, they wouldn't have touched it. Then God would have let them live forever. Seeing they disobeyed Him, and ate of the tree, He knew He could not trust them; so they would have to die and go back to the dust from which He had taken them. What a sad day that was.

How much was at stake in that little test! If only they had known!

Alas, they failed the test. Both of them. And no sooner had they eaten of the fruit than they knew something was the matter. Something had gone wrong. For the first time in their lives they felt worried. What would God think of them? they wondered. What would He say to them?

Then came fear. As the day dragged wearily on, and evening shadows lengthened, they talked in frightened whispers. Somehow all happiness had suddenly gone out of their lives. For the first time they felt sad, miserable, wretched. There was no joy for them in Eden any more. They wanted only to run away and hide.

What a pity! But isn't this the result of disobedience even today? It just spoils everything, doesn't it?

STORY 5

The Price of Sin

I T WAS beginning to get dark. Already a cool breeze was rustling the leaves of the trees. Soon it would be night, and the stars would appear again.

But there was no happiness in Eden on this lovely evening. With bowed heads and aching hearts Adam and Eve wandered sadly through the forest glades where but a little while before they had known such perfect joy.

Suddenly they heard a familiar sound. It was the voice of God as He walked "in the garden in the cool of the day."

Until now they had rejoiced to hear this wondrous voice, running toward it as to that of a much-loved friend. Now they ran away from it. "And Adam and his wife hid themselves from the presence of the Lord God amongst the trees of the garden."

It was a foolish thing to do. They could not hide from God —any more than you or I could hide from Him today.

"And the Lord God called unto Adam, and said unto him, Where art thou?"

God did not need to ask. He knew where they were. But He wanted them to know that He was looking for them, that He still cared for them and loved them.

What tenderness there was in His voice at that moment! He seemed to be saying, "Why are you hiding from One who loves you so? Why don't you come to meet Me as you used to do?"

Unable to keep silent any longer, Adam stepped slowly from his hiding place and said, "I heard thy voice in the garden, and I was afraid."

Afraid! What a strange thing for him to say! He had never been afraid before. He had never known what fear was. Now this grand, noble being, God's masterpiece of creation, was afraid. And, oh, most sorrowful thought, he was afraid of His Maker!

But this is what sin does. It makes a person fear even his best friends. It turns the bravest man into a coward. It bows the noblest head in shame.

God knew what had happened, of course, for nothing is hidden from Him. But He asked Adam, "Hast thou eaten of the tree, whereof I commanded thee that thou shouldest not eat?"

Yes, Adam had eaten of the tree. So had Eve. Both were guilty of grave disobedience. Sadly they stood before God, wondering what He would say next, what their penalty would be.

God had warned them, "In the day that thou eatest thereof, dying thou shalt die." And they had often wondered what He had meant by those strange words. Never having seen death, they could not tell what it was like. Now were they to die?

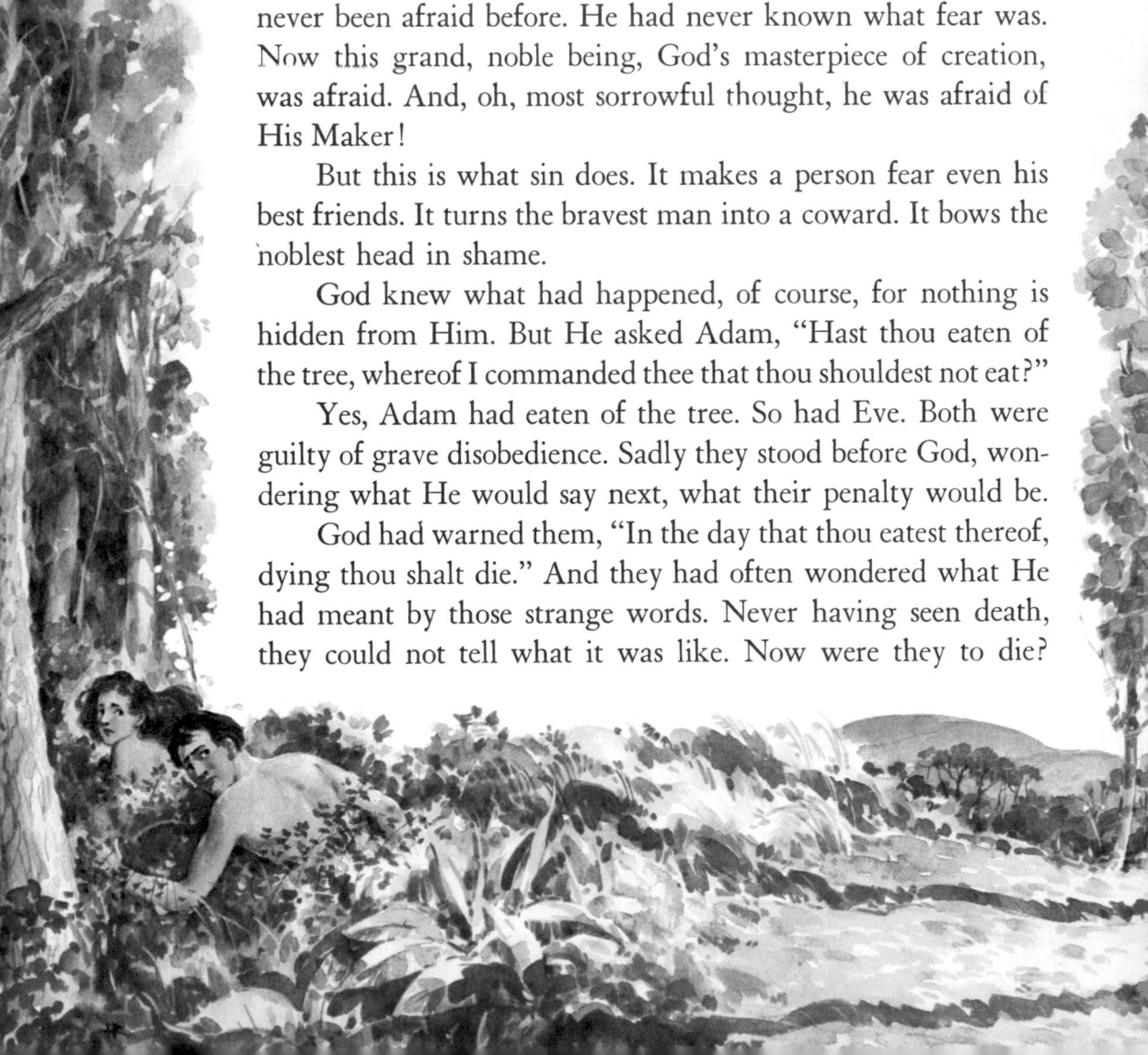

Would today be their last day upon the earth? How sad! They had been here such a little while.

Then it was that God told them what must happen to them because of their sin. He explained how, from the very moment of their disobedience, they had begun to die. And in their hearts they knew it was true.

They could not live forever as He had planned they should. Eternal life was not for them. Not now. Dying they must die, returning at last to the dust of which He had made them. It would take a long time, many hundreds of years, in fact, but at last this would be their fate.

Meanwhile, they would have to leave their beautiful home. Instead of the pleasant, easy time they had been having, they would have to work hard and long for their living. They would know pain and sorrow. They would learn the awfulness of sin as they saw all nature suffer with them because of what they had done.

Looking at Adam in deepest pity, God said, "Because thou hast hearkened unto the voice of thy wife, and hast eaten of the tree, of which I commanded thee, saying, Thou shalt not eat of it: cursed is the ground for thy sake; in sorrow shalt thou eat of it all the days of thy life: thorns also and thistles shall it bring forth to thee; and thou shalt eat the herb of the field; in the sweat of thy face shalt thou eat bread, till thou return unto the ground; for out of it wast thou taken: for dust thou art, and unto dust shalt thou return."

Was God too hard on them? No. He knew the deadly nature of sin, how it wrecks and spoils everything it touches.

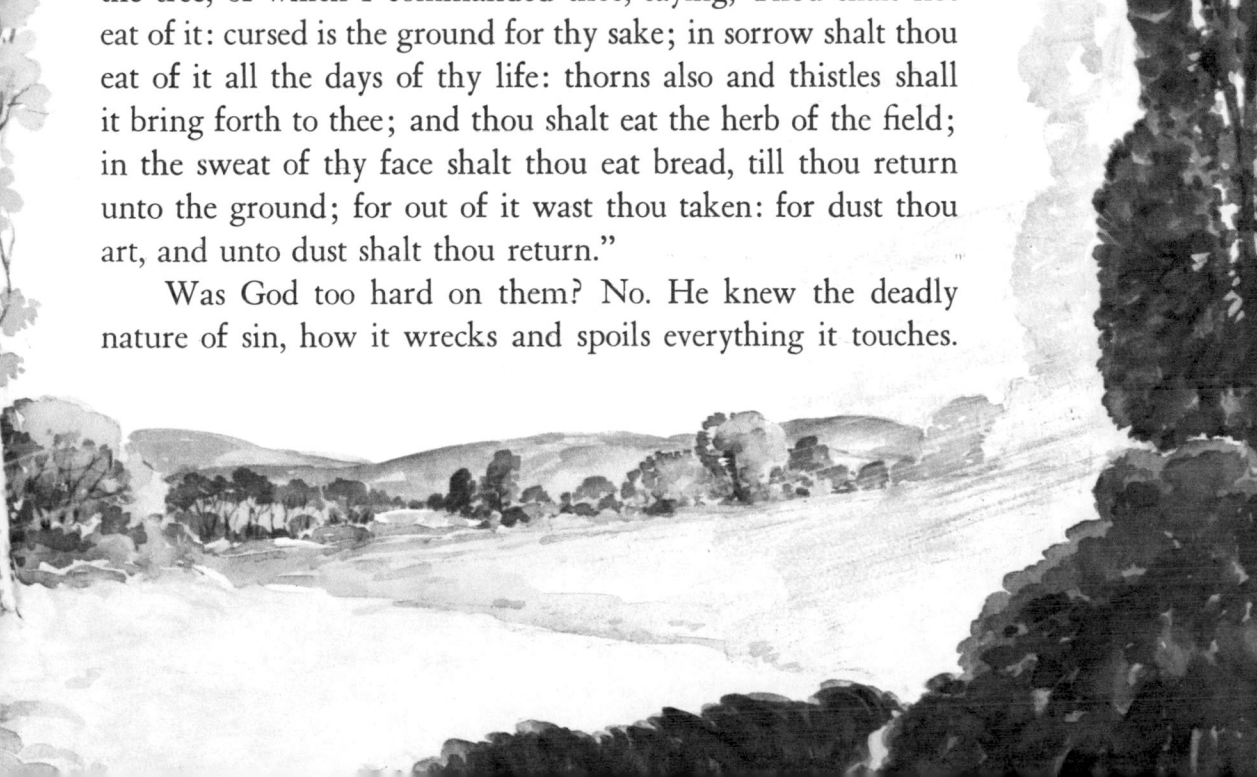

He had seen it break the sweet harmony of heaven. Now it was beginning again on earth, threatening to ruin this glorious Paradise He had only just created. Something had to be done. Adam and Eve must be made to realize what sin means, what it does, and what it costs.

It was all very sad, and I don't know who felt worse as the two poor things turned from God and began to walk away from their beautiful Eden home.

Darkness was gathering, and from out of the forest peered many animal friends, their wonder-filled eyes seeming to ask each other, What is the matter? Where are they going? Even the birds hushed their twittering as they listened in awe to the great, heartbroken sobs of their lord and master as he and his lovely wife walked out into the night.

For Adam and Eve the hardest to bear was the thought that they could not return. By morning Eden would be only a memory. They would never enter it again.

Turning to take one last look at all they had loved and lost, they saw a strange light glowing in the darkness along the way that they had come. It seemed like a fiery weapon held in an angel's hand. And the flaming sword "turned every way, to keep the way of the tree of life."

The way was closed; the gate was locked. So great is the cost of one little sin!

STORY 6

One Gleam of Hope

HOW FAR Adam and Eve wandered from their Eden home we are not told, but they soon noticed many changes.

For one thing they found that they needed clothes, and we read that "the Lord God" made "coats of skins, and clothed them."

What wonderful coats these must have been, made with all the skill, all the thoughtfulness, all the tender pity of man's Creator!

Yet these coats meant death. At least one animal, possibly two, had to die that Adam and Eve might live. And so the cost of sin was brought home to them again.

Many times on their journeyings they must have talked of the good old days they had enjoyed in the glorious Paradise God had given them in the beginning. Many times too they must have wondered whether they would ever be allowed to see it again.

73

ONE GLEAM OF HOPE

As again and again they went over all that had happened on that sad day when they had made their terrible mistake, one thing kept coming back to their minds. It was something God had said to the serpent.

Over and over they repeated it, wondering just what it might mean: "I will put enmity between thee and the woman, and between thy seed and her seed; it shall bruise thy head, and thou shalt bruise his heel."

Whatever could this mean?

One thing was certain: It meant that Eve would have children, and she was glad of that. But how much more did it mean?

Well, there would be "enmity," or war, between Eve's children and the serpent's children.

Eve knew that she would never forgive the serpent for the way he had deceived her and robbed her of her lovely home; nor would her children. She would see to that. And surely, when God said to the serpent, "It shall bruise thy head," it meant that her seed, her children—or one of them—would win the conflict at last.

Here for the first time she saw a gleam of hope. Someday the wicked serpent, who had brought such sorrow and loss upon her and her husband, would be destroyed. Then, perhaps, God would let them go back to Eden.

How they both loved this promise! It was the first promise ever made to man, and the first one mentioned in the Bible. To Adam and Eve it was the *only* promise they had, and how precious it must have been to them! On dark days, when everything seemed to go wrong, they remembered it and talked about

75

Adam and Eve often talked about the promise God made to them just before they were driven out of the Garden of Eden. Eve clearly remembered how God cursed the serpent, and why.

it till hope sprang up in their sorrowing hearts once more.

You can imagine how eagerly they looked forward to having their first baby. Perhaps *he* would be the one—when he grew up—to bruise the serpent's head. Perhaps they wouldn't have to wait very long to return to Eden after all!

But when Cain was born he did not crush the serpent. Instead he turned out to be a big disappointment. Nor did Abel, or Seth, or any of their children fulfill the promise.

So the years went by, and still no one came to restore them to Paradise and the tree of life. It must have been hard to keep on hoping.

What was it that the Lord had in mind when He made that promise in the garden? To whom did He refer when He spoke of the Seed of the woman? He was thinking, of course, of His Son, and how one day He would come to the earth as a baby—one of Eve's children— and fight the great enemy Himself. As Jesus Christ, Emmanuel, "God with us," He would destroy Satan and bring Adam and Eve and all who love God back to Eden.

Of course, if God had said to Adam and Eve, "You will have to wait thousands of years before you see your home again," they would have been much discouraged. So He told them just enough to let them know that all would be well at last. This cheered their poor, sad hearts, and led them to keep on hoping. And men have passed on the same blessed hope from one to another down the ages.

This is how it came about that all the people who loved God —even in those far-off times—began looking forward to the

coming of Jesus. This is why Enoch, "the seventh from Adam," said, "Behold, the Lord cometh with ten thousands of his saints, to execute judgment upon all."

Today the same hope is ours. Everywhere boys and girls who love Jesus are looking eagerly for His return. For when He comes the promise that God made to Adam will be fulfilled, and "that old serpent, called the Devil," will be destroyed. Then, too, Eden, beautiful, glorious Eden, will be restored, and the children of God will live there in perfect happiness forever.

STORY 7

The First Baby

WHEN God created the fish, birds, and animals He said to them, "Be fruitful, and multiply."

In answer to His command there soon appeared in the rivers and the seas thousands of baby fish, from tiny minnows to infant whales and sea lions. In the trees and bushes of the forest, birds of every kind and color began to build nests, lay eggs, and hatch them, as birds have done through all the centuries from that day to this.

To the first sheep came the first little lambs, to the first bears came cuddly little cubs, to the first elephants came cute little baby elephants—and so on through all creation. The whole world became one vast nursery, with thousands of mothers and fathers doing their best to feed and train their children.

To Adam and Eve also God said, "Be fruitful, and multiply." He did not want them to be alone. He planned that they should have a large family and enjoy the love and companionship of many, many boys and girls.

79

The first family was a busy one. Father Adam cultivated the soil, his boys learned how to plant the seeds that grew and provided them food to eat, and Mother Eve kept the home.

When you stop to think of it this was by far the greatest gift of God's love to these dear creatures of His hand. Better than all the beauties of nature, better than all the rich stores of gold and silver in the earth, better than all the friendship of the animals, was the power to have boys and girls who would one day grow up to be men and women like themselves.

This most precious gift was intended to bring them endless happiness, as their children and their children's children should come to love and honor them through all time to come.

How many children Adam and Eve had we do not know. But in view of what we are told of those far-off days, we may be sure they had lots and lots of them. And what bright and beautiful children they must have been, offspring of these two majestic beings formed by the Creator Himself!

How the hills and dales must have rung with their happy laughter as they romped together in the fields and woods and played with their animal friends! Beyond doubt it was the joy and love of these dear children that helped Adam and Eve bear up under their sorrow at the loss of Eden.

Of all their children we know the names of only three—and these all boys. Of course, they must have had girls in their family too, but none of their names is to be found in the Bible.

The name of their first baby—the first ever born on this earth—was Cain. No wonder we know *that* name, for first babies are always so very, very important, aren't they?

How Adam and Eve must have loved that little boy! How they must have counted his fingers and toes and marveled at the beauty of his eyes, his nose, his ears, his mouth, time and

80

time again, just as all fathers and mothers have admired their first babies ever since!

I feel sure too that the Son of God took many a tender look at that soft little bundle of loveliness in Eve's arms, for He knew that someday He would come to live among the children of Adam just like that.

What a comfort little Cain must have been to the sad hearts of his parents! The very joy of looking at him, playing with him, and loving him must have helped them forget their sorrows. And as they thought of the day when he would grow up to be a fine big boy, a young man just like his noble father, what wonderful dreams they must have dreamed for him, what great hopes for the future they must have cherished in their hearts for this first-born son!

Alas, it was not to be!

Instead, this dear, dear treasure, this joy of their hearts, became the source of their greatest sorrow.

They thought they had paid the price of sin when they were driven from the Garden of Eden. But they had only begun to pay it. Soon, all too soon, they were to see what sin can do in a boy's life, what it can do to a boy's home, what it can do to his parents' hearts.

Oh, sad, sad story! This beautiful baby, this perfect child, first-born of the world's first man and woman, became the world's first murderer!

STORY 8

The First Quarrel

THE SECOND little boy whose name is found in the Bible was Abel. He was born fairly soon after Cain, for the two grew up together.

They must have played in the woods and paddled in the streams together. Perhaps they were the first little boys to make a boat and float it on the nearest pond.

What a wonderful time they had in those far-off days when the world was young and so very, very beautiful!

These two boys were probably leaders in their large and ever-growing family. Younger brothers and sisters looked up to them and followed their example, which is no doubt why their names and none of the others are recorded. Because they were leaders, the way they lived and acted became very important.

As time went on, and the boys grew to manhood, they turned to different interests. Cain loved to grow things. The Bible says he was "a tiller of the ground." Probably he invented the first plow. And how thrilled he must have been to gather

83

While Cain and Abel were both offering sacrifices on their altars God sent fire from heaven and accepted Abel's offering. This made Cain jealous and angry with his brother.

seeds, and sow them, and watch them grow into strong, sturdy, beautiful plants.

Abel, we are told, preferred to work with animals. He became "a keeper of sheep"—the first shepherd—and I imagine he took most loving care of the first wee lambs.

Both boys had been told about God. Most of Eve's bedtime stories were probably about Eden and all that happened there, for those glorious days in that wonderful garden were her most precious memories. So these two boys, as well as all her children, learned of the loving Creator, of the devil's subtle temptation, of how she yielded to it, and of all the sad things that happened afterward. Best loved of all Eve's stories was the one about God's promise that someday one of her children would crush the serpent's head and lead the family back to their Eden home. Every child must have hoped that he might be that hero.

The children learned too that they should give offerings to God to show their love and respect for Him and their faith in His promise to help them. Time and again they were told that sin is so hateful that only by death—the shedding of blood—can it be purged away.

"In process of time . . . Cain brought of the fruit of the ground an offering unto the Lord. And Abel, he also brought of the firstlings of his flock and of the fat thereof. And the Lord had respect unto Abel and to his offering: but unto Cain and to his offering he had not respect."

Just how God showed "respect" to Abel's offering, the Bible does not say. It may well be that fire came down from heaven upon Abel's dead little lamb and consumed it. Anyway,

there was a difference. It was clear that Cain's offering of fruits, nuts, and vegetables was not welcome.

Why did God make this difference? Why did He have "respect" to one offering and not to the other?

Because by shedding the blood of a lamb Abel revealed that he understood God's plan to defeat Satan and win back for man his Eden home—that it could only be by the death of "the Lamb of God," the very Son of God Himself.

Cain no doubt understood this just as well as Abel, but he couldn't see why his offering would not do just as well as his brother's. And when he saw that God had "respect" to Abel's offering, while ignoring his own, he was filled with jealousy.

"And Cain was very wroth, and his countenance fell"; that is, he looked as he felt—very angry indeed.

God saw those ugly looks—as He sees all ugly looks today —and He said to Cain, "Why art thou wroth? and why is thy countenance fallen? If thou doest well, shalt thou not be accepted? and if thou doest not well, sin lieth at the door."

God was trying to be fair. He wasn't playing favorites. Cain had just the same chance as Abel. Had he brought the same offering, God would gladly have accepted it as He had accepted Abel's.

But Cain was in no mood to be reasoned with. He was so angry he couldn't see straight. He thought that he was right and God was wrong. And he was sure Abel had played some trick to win God's favor.

By and by he went over to where Abel was standing in the field and "talked with Abel his brother." What he said we have

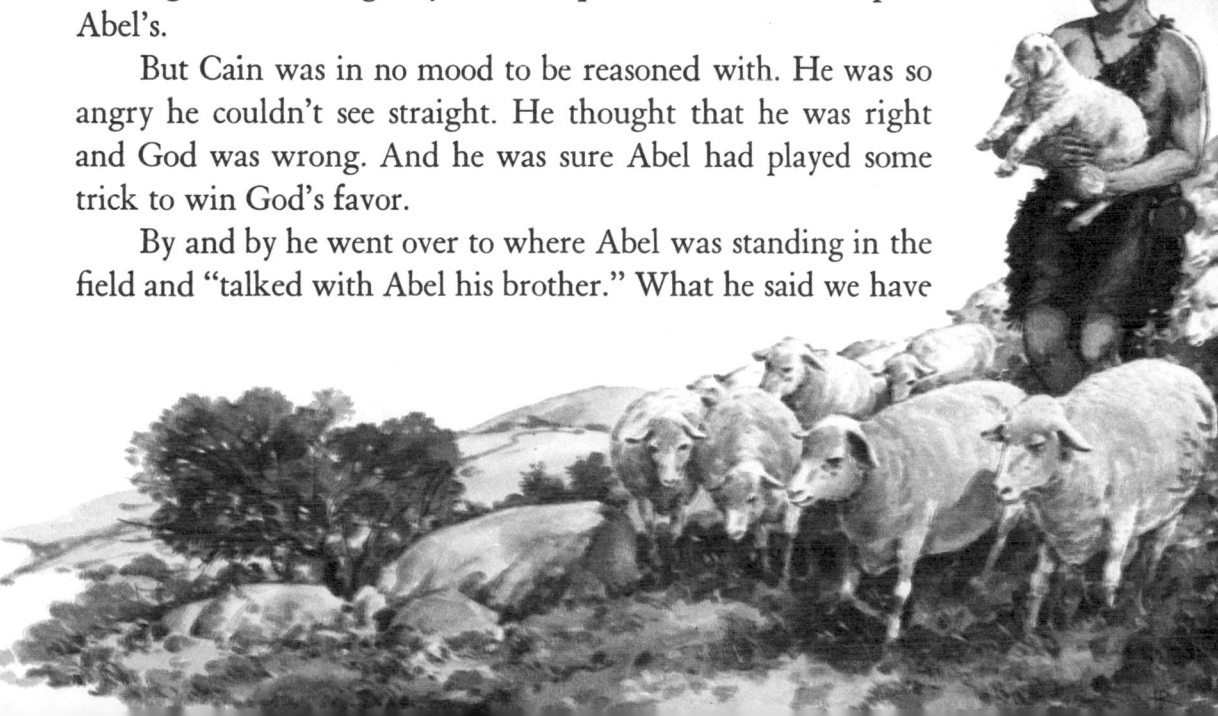

not been told. But we can be sure it was nothing pleasant or brotherly. His voice rose. He called names. He made false charges. It was the first quarrel.

More and more angry did Cain become until at last he "rose up against Abel his brother, and slew him."

Whether he struck him with his fist, or a club, or stabbed him with a knife the Bible doesn't say. We are left with a picture of that tall, handsome youth sagging limply to the ground.

Death had come to the human family. The first home had been broken for the first time.

Oh, sad, sad day!

Who brought the news to Adam and Eve nobody knows, but the shock to them must have been terrible. I can see them running out to that bloodstained field, picking up the poor, stiffening body, unable to believe it would never breathe, never smile, never speak to them again. And I can hear the heartbroken sobs of that poor father and mother as they cried, as David did long afterward for Absalom: "O my son Abel, my son, my son Abel! Would God I had died for thee, O Abel, my son, my son!"

STORY 9

The Marked Man

CAIN was terrified at what he had done. As he saw his brother's body collapse upon the ground, he wondered what had happened, for he had never seen a man die before. Then, as the awful truth dawned upon him that Abel was dead—dead like that lamb on the altar which had been the cause of all the trouble—his anger turned to fear and remorse.

He couldn't go back home, not now. He couldn't face father and mother. Not after doing this dreadful thing. Nor could he face his brothers and sisters, for they would be angry with him and perhaps would want to kill him as he had killed Abel. He would have to run away as far as he could go, and never come back.

That is what sin does. It separates loved ones, wrecks happiness, drives peace from the mind and joy from the heart.

As Cain fled from the scene he heard God calling to him, "Where is Abel thy brother?"

"I know not," said Cain, as though he could deceive God. Then, insolently, "Am I my brother's keeper?"

"What hast thou done?" said God. "The voice of thy brother's blood crieth unto me from the ground."

Of course God knew all the time what had happened. Nothing is hid from Him. He had witnessed the dreadful deed. He had seen Abel's blood upon the ground, and it cried for justice. Indeed, in the silence and helplessness of death Abel cried louder than if he had been alive that something be done about this great wrong.

Cain had broken the sixth commandment of God's holy law: "Thou shalt not kill." But by his pride, his jealousy, his anger, his selfishness, his lying, he had broken all the other nine as well. He had to be punished. But how?

"And now art thou cursed from the earth," said God. "When thou tillest the ground, it shall not henceforth yield unto thee her strength; a fugitive and a vagabond shalt thou be in the earth."

In His mercy God did not take Cain's life, but sent him away from his home and from all who had been so dear to him—

just as He had sent Adam and Eve from the Garden of Eden when *they* had sinned against Him. The lad was to be a fugitive, forever running for his life, a vagabond, a "tramp," who never dared settle down.

"My punishment is greater than I can bear," cried Cain as he realized what his sin had cost him. "Behold, thou hast driven me out this day from the face of the earth; and from thy face shall I be hid; and I shall be a fugitive and a vagabond in the earth; and it shall come to pass, that every one that findeth me shall slay me."

Poor Cain pictured himself as forever living in constant fear of his life, always fleeing farther and farther from the home to which he could never return. Out of pity for this youth who had been so dear to Him from babyhood, God "set a mark upon Cain, lest any finding him should kill him."

Just what this mark was the Bible does not say. It may well have been a change in his face that sin, remorse, and worry always bring. Whatever it was, from this moment on he was a different man, the first marked man in history. Marked, not that he might be caught and punished, but marked by his punishment that he might be spared.

The mark did something else. It reminded Cain, his wife, his children, and all who should ever meet him how awful are the results of sin. It was a warning to all never to follow that evil course which had brought so much sorrow upon himself and his loved ones.

"And Cain went out from the presence of the Lord, and dwelt in the land of Nod, on the east of Eden."

Did you ever stop to think what that meant to Adam and Eve?

In one brief day they lost two sons. Abel was dead; and Cain, their first-born, on whom they had depended so much, and on whom they had pinned their hopes for the future, was an outcast, hurrying toward the unknown lands toward the east for fear of his life.

What a dark day that must have been! Not since that awful night when they had taken their last look at Eden, and seen the angel with the flaming sword barring their return, had they felt such utter loneliness and despair.

Well might they have wondered whether life was worth living and what was the use of hoping any more.

Yct hope came again to their poor, sad hearts. And, as so often happens, it came in the form of a baby, for it was at this very time that Eve had another little boy. The Bible says, "And she bare a son, and called his name Seth: For God, said she, hath appointed me another seed instead of Abel, whom Cain slew."

So they started again, believing and hoping that this might be the baby through whom the promised seed would come. And this time, though they did not know it, they were right.

STORY 10

Adam's Last Birthday

WHEN that little boy Seth was born Adam was 130 years old. That sounds very old to us, but it wasn't old in those days. Indeed, Adam was then only at the beginning of his life. He lived eight hundred years after that.

It may seem hard to believe, but on Adam's last birthday he was 930 years old. If he had had a birthday cake as you do, with candles on it, what a sight it would have been!

Perhaps you are saying, "Nobody could have lived that long!" But wait a minute. Remember, Adam was the first man, created by God Himself on the sixth day of creation week. He was, therefore, the most perfectly formed man who ever lived. His heart, his lungs, his muscles, fresh from God's own hands, were made to last forever. Indeed, they *would* have lasted forever had he not sinned. But for his one sad mistake he could have eaten of the tree of life and lived on and on and on.

Besides, in the beginning of the world's history there were none of the diseases so common now, which cause so many people to die very young. For hundreds of years Adam probably never knew what it was to be sick. Most likely he never had a cold, or mumps, or measles, or chicken pox, or even a toothache. So wonderfully had God made him that he kept his marvelous health and strength for most of his long, long life. Only old age weakened him, causing him at last, as God warned him in Eden, to lie down and die, and so return to the dust from which he had been made.

Now, if Adam lived to be over nine hundred years old, as I am sure he did, then he must have seen not only his sons grow to manhood but also his grandsons, his great-grandsons, and his great-great-grandsons.

By the time he died he must have been a great-great-great-great-great grandfather. I really don't know how many "greats" to put in. If perchance he celebrated his nine hundred and thirtieth birthday by inviting all his relatives, thousands upon thousands of people must have been there.

You see, if all these people were descended from Adam, as of course they were, they were all related to each other—brothers and sisters, uncles and aunts, nephews and nieces, cousins and half cousins. Thus the population of the earth in that far-off day was made up of one big family, with Adam the grand old father of them all.

But not only did Adam live a long time. So did his children. Seth, that little boy who came to cheer his heart after he lost both Cain and Abel, lived to be 912. And one of Seth's sons, called Enos, lived to be 905.

Others who lived a long, long time were Cainan, 910 years;

Mahalaleel, 895; and Jared, 962. The man who lived longest of all was Methuselah, who lived to be 969—almost a thousand. Then there was Lamech, 777, and Noah, 950.

You can read about these grand old men in the fifth chapter of the book of Genesis. And when you do, take a pencil and paper and draw lines to show how long each of them lived. Allow half an inch to a hundred years. Work it out carefully, and you will discover some very interesting facts.

First, you will notice that of the nine patriarchs mentioned in this chapter, eight of them lived at the same time as Adam. Only Noah never saw him.

Second, you will see that two of them, Methuselah and Lamech, not only knew Adam personally, but lived almost to the time of the Flood.

Third, you will see that Noah was 600 years old when the Flood came, and lived 350 years after it.

And what does this mean? It means that everybody in those far-off days must have known about the story of creation. Everybody must have known about Eden, and God's wonderful goodness to Adam and Eve in that glorious garden He made for them. Everybody must have known too about their temptation and fall. And, most important of all, everybody must have known about God's promise to redeem and restore all that Adam and Eve so carelessly threw away.

From father to son, from one patriarch to another, the wonderful story was handed down, so that there was never any excuse for sin, never a reason why anyone should not know God and love Him with all his heart.

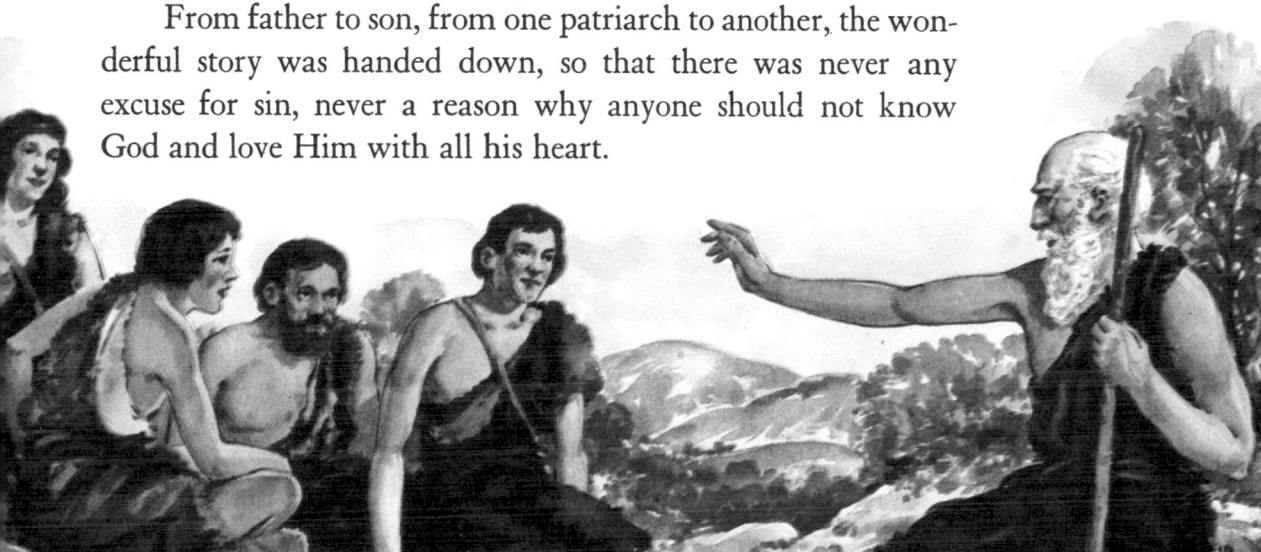

STORY 11

The Man Who Walked Into Heaven

IF YOU drew those lines I suggested, you will see that one line is much shorter than all the others. It is the line marking the life of Enoch. His father lived to be 962 years old, and his son 969, but he lived only 365 years.

Why was this? Did he get ill and die early?

No, he didn't. In fact, he didn't die at all. That is the wonderful thing about Enoch. The Bible says, "God took him," which means God took him away without his having to die.

That is something to think about. God does not treat everybody like this. Indeed, so far as we know, only two people in all the history of the world—Enoch and Elijah—were taken like this without dying.

Why did God take Enoch? There must have been a very good reason for making an exception in his case. There must have been something about this man that made God love him more than all the other people of his day.

95

Enoch was a very good man. He loved God and was kind and helpful to his neighbors. He often went into the woods to talk with God in the cool shade and quiet of the trees.

You may say, But did not God love Adam, His masterpiece of creation, very, very dearly? He did. But God let Adam die, just as He said He would, after he had lived 930 years.

How about Seth? Wasn't he specially beloved too? He was. But God let him die also, after he had lived 912 years. And so with all the others. God loved them, but He let them die.

With Enoch, however, it was different. God loved him so much He couldn't let him die. So He took him away to live with Him forever.

Why? The Bible doesn't tell us very much about it, but just enough so we may understand. It says: "And Enoch lived sixty and five years, and begat Methuselah: and Enoch walked with God after he begat Methuselah three hundred years. . . . And Enoch walked with God: and he was not; for God took him."

There is the secret! He walked with God. That is what God wanted Adam to do from the very beginning. There wasn't anything God wouldn't have done for Adam had he walked with Him as Enoch did, instead of forgetting Him and wandering away. Certainly he never would have died.

And so with Seth, Enos, Cainan, and all the rest. God wanted them all to walk with Him, but none of them quite came up to His expectations.

Only Enoch. He was different from the others. He loved God with all his heart. He had one purpose: to serve God and do His will. He thought about God all day long, striving in every word and deed to please Him. Never was there any selfishness, greediness, jealousy, or anger in his heart, for he believed

96

that such wicked thoughts were unworthy of a child of God.

No wonder God was drawn to this dear man. Indeed, I can almost hear God saying, "Here is a man after My own heart. He is just what I hoped all the sons of Adam would be like. Dear Enoch! What a noble, godly soul!"

"And Enoch walked with God . . . three hundred years."

That was a long time; but God was testing him, watching him every day, every moment. And the more God watched him, the more He loved him. Day by day, week by week, month by month, century by century, Enoch walked with God until at last, instead of dying, he just kept on walking right into heaven!

What was it made Enoch want to live such a life as this? It may have been the result of a talk he had with Adam, for Adam, remember, was still alive in Enoch's day. Perhaps as he learned more of the love of God in making the world and man, he made up his mind to love God sincerely in return. And yet it might have happened because of something else.

The Bible says that Enoch walked with God "after he

begat Methuselah"; that is, after his little boy was born. Having a little boy means a lot to most daddies, and it could well be that, as Enoch looked lovingly upon that precious baby of his, and thought of the wonderful goodness of God in giving him a child like himself, that he gave his heart to God as never before and promised to love and serve Him all his life.

Be that as it may, from that moment Enoch walked with God, which means they kept in step. And as they walked together they must have talked to each other—"secrets" too— things God could not reveal to anybody else.

That is when Enoch learned so much of God's plans for the future, and why he was able to write that great prophecy: "Behold, the Lord cometh with ten thousands of his saints." Even though he was only "the seventh from Adam," God helped him to see clear down the ages to that wondrous day when Jesus shall come in His glory.

And so, after three hundred years of walking with God like this, "God took him." In the New Testament we read that "Enoch was translated that he should not see death; . . . for before his translation he had this testimony, that he pleased God."

Isn't that a beautiful record for a man to leave behind him? "He pleased God." Could that be said of you? Do you try to please Him every day? Always?

It's a wonderful thing to walk with God, seeking to please Him in every thought and word and deed. And if we do, who knows, perhaps someday, like Enoch, we too shall go walking right on into heaven.

PART III

Stories About Noah and the Flood

(GENESIS 6:1-11:9)

PART THREE

STORY 1

Sad, Bad Days

WHILE Enoch walked with God most of Adam's children and grandchildren did not. They walked by themselves and forgot all about Him. They became selfish and greedy, quarrelsome and cruel. They began to fight among themselves and kill each other, even as Cain had killed Abel.

It is hard to understand how such things could have happened such a short time after creation, and such a little way from all the peace and harmony of Eden. Yet it is not uncommon even today for boys and girls to be cross and unruly right after church. Some can become real little pests just as soon as a nice picnic is over. It doesn't take long for some to forget kindness and love that they should remember forever.

So it was back there in the early days of the world. As people drifted farther and farther from God, they drifted farther and farther into sin.

Satan who, in the form of a serpent, had deceived Adam

101

There were no churches in Enoch's day. Those who loved God built stone altars and there worshiped. When men became wicked, they neglected God's altars and fought one another.

and Eve in the garden, rejoiced at the turn of events. He had schemed to spoil God's plans for a happy and beautiful world, and now he was succeeding better than he had dared to hope. Having heard God's promise that the Seed of the woman should bruise his head, he made up his mind that nothing of the sort should ever happen.

The best way to do this, he thought, would be to lead as many as possible of Adam's children to disobey God and do all sorts of things displeasing to Him. So he began to tempt them in many ways, and all who were not living close to God fell for his deceptions.

Adam and Eve, having learned the costliness of sin from their own sad experience, tried their best to warn their wayward boys and girls of their danger, and persuade them to follow the good way "which leadeth unto life." Year after year and century after century they stood against the rising tide of evil. But it was a losing struggle. The wicked became ever bolder in their wickedness. More and more openly they mocked at Adam's counsel, sneering that he was too old-fashioned to understand young people, and grumbling every time he tried to make them keep good rules.

Adam lived to see his once beautiful and peaceful world inhabited by a host of very sinful people. Just before he died he heard Enoch, the man who walked with God, rebuke the "ungodly deeds" of the "murmurers" and "complainers, walking after their own lusts."

That was about nine hundred years after creation. Five hundred years later things had become much worse. By this time there was quarreling and fighting everywhere. Nobody's life was safe. The Bible says, "The earth was filled with violence."

How sad that it should have been so! God had done so much to make the world a place of beauty, peace, and joy. Now Satan had almost ruined everything.

How sorry God must have been! The Bible says that "God saw that the wickedness of man was great in the earth, and that every imagination of the thoughts of his heart was only evil continually. And it repented the Lord that he had made man on the earth, and *it grieved him at his heart.*"

In those last few words we catch a glimpse of the depths of His sorrow. He was thinking of what might have been if only Adam and Eve had not listened to the serpent, if only all their children had loved Him, and walked with Him, as Enoch had done!

With awful sadness God said to Himself, "I will destroy man whom I have created from the face of the earth; both man, and beast, and the creeping thing, and the fowls of the air; for it repenteth me that I have made them."

Conditions must have become very terrible indeed for God to say that. How it must have hurt Him to think of destroying all His creatures and all the beautiful things He had made such a little time before!

Yet even now His heart of infinite love held back from carrying out so dreadful a judgment, necessary though it was. Perhaps there were still some who would turn back to Him if they were given one more chance. If there were but a handful, even two or three, He would gladly wait.

"My spirit shall not always strive with man," He said; "yet his days shall be an hundred and twenty years."

In other words, He would wait that long, a hundred and twenty years, to see whether any would heed His call to repentance.

But now, if such a call was to be given, somebody must be found to give it. But who? With most of Adam's children following the ways of Satan, who could be trusted with so important a task? Was there anyone left through whom God could speak His last message of mercy to a doomed world?

≋≋≋≋≋

STORY 2

God's Shipbuilder

≋≋≋≋≋≋≋≋≋≋

LOOKING for someone to tell the people what He was planning to do, God thought of Noah, last of the ten old patriarchs, now nearly five hundred years old.

Keen, alert, and vigorous, he was one of the wisest men of his day. Moreover, amid all the evil about him, he remained loyal to God and the right. The Bible says, "Noah was a just man and perfect in his generations, and Noah walked with God."

In this he was like Enoch, and no doubt this is why God chose him for his most important task and finally saved him and his family from the Flood.

Just what Noah's usual work was we are not told. Perhaps he was a farmer, like so many of his relatives. But he may have been a builder, perhaps even a boatbuilder, for by this time people surely had boats of many kinds on their beautiful lakes and rivers. Certainly he was a great designer, or he never could have carried out God's instructions for building the ark.

105

One day—one of the great days in history—God came to Noah and said, "The end of all flesh is come before me; for the earth is filled with violence. . . . Behold, I, even I, do bring a flood of waters upon the earth, to destroy all flesh, wherein is the breath of life, from under heaven; and every thing that is in the earth shall die."

This must have saddened the old man. He knew the people about him were very wicked, that they needed to be punished, but the destruction of everybody and the whole beautiful world —that was something too dreadful to think about.

But even as God spoke of punishment He told of a way out that all could take if they wished.

"Make thee an ark of gopher wood," He said.

An ark! That meant something that would float. A ship, as we would say. But would it be large enough to hold all who might want to find refuge in it?

Noah must have been amazed at the figures God gave him to work on. It was no small lifeboat that He had in mind, but a huge vessel, big as a modern battleship. It was to be 600 feet long, 100 feet wide, and 60 feet in height—almost as big as some of the ocean liners today. The *United States,* pride of the U.S. merchant fleet, is 990 feet long, 101 feet 6 inches wide, and 122 feet from keel to top. It has 12 decks and a crew of 1,000. In war it could carry 14,000 soldiers.

GOD'S SHIPBUILDER

Why did God ask Noah to build so large a vessel? First, because He wanted every single soul to know there was room for him in the ark if he wished to be saved. Second, because He planned to preserve a great number of birds and animals in it. And third, because He knew it would have to ride out the worst storms and the roughest seas of all time.

After Noah was alone he must have thought a long time about what God had asked him to do. What a lot of trees would have to be cut down and hauled to the building site! Imagine all the sawing, planing, and shaping that would have to be done. And all the men who would have to be hired—and paid! It was a huge task for any man to tackle.

And then Noah must have wondered what everybody would think when they saw him building a ship six hundred feet long! Most likely they would say he was out of his mind, throwing his money away on a crazy idea. But "thus did Noah according to all that God commanded him, so did he." People do just that, regardless of what others may think of them, when they are walking with God.

So Noah started to work, drawing the plans, preparing the lumber, and laying the keel.

At first the neighbors probably didn't take much notice. But as the years went by, and one by one the great wooden ribs of the vessel were secured in place, and it became clear that it was a ship and not a barn that he was building, they began to make fun of him. How they laughed! For they could see

no reason for building any such thing. What would anybody want with a boat this big? And they probably felt quite sure it wouldn't float, anyway, even if Noah could get it into the water.

Noah tried to explain, but it was no use. As people flocked to watch him work he warned them of the Flood that was coming, and how God had told him to build a place of refuge for those who wanted to be saved.

The more he tried to explain, however, the more they mocked him. But he went on building and preaching, just the same, while the years, the last few years of that beautiful world, slipped away.

≈≈≈≈≈≈

STORY 3

The Animals Move In

≈≈≈≈≈≈≈≈

I T IS the hundred and twentieth year since Noah started to build the ark. The great ship is finished.

Sixty feet high and six hundred feet long, it has become a landmark, visible for miles in every direction.

Everybody knows about it, although all have become so used to it they don't even bother to go near it anymore. They only point at it with a smile and say, "Noah's folly!"

The vast ship itself looks gaunt and deserted, for only Noah remains with it, and his family. All the hired workmen have left. They just worked for their pay, and now, the job over, they have gone home. They never really believed Noah's message.

The great door of the ark stands open, as if inviting everybody to enter and find safety. But nobody comes.

There is a strange silence everywhere, broken only by the sound of echoing feet as Noah and his sons walk through the empty vessel, making sure that all is firm and strong and watertight.

For 120 years the old
patriarch has preached of coming destruction,
but now nowhere is so peaceful as here around the
ark. Not even the sound of a saw or a hammer can be heard.

Could it be that Noah has made a mistake? Could he have
misunderstood what God said to him? Perhaps nothing will
happen after all. Perhaps he has wasted his time and money.
Perhaps the ark will just rot away where it stands.

But look! Something *is* happening! See! Those animals
over there! They seem to be walking toward the ark. They are.
And now others are coming from all directions. What can
it mean?

Now people are running to watch the amazing sight, as
animals of every kind, evidently guided by some invisible hand,
make their way to the ark, climb up the ramp, and in through
the open door.

Great elephants are lumbering up the creaking timbers,
followed by growling tigers, grunting bears, and bleating sheep.

THE ANIMALS MOVE IN

Behind them are zebras, antelopes, kangaroos, pandas, donkeys, goats, and a host of others, while squirrels, opossums, beavers, chipmunks, and all sorts of little creatures go scurrying along in between.

What a sight! Nothing like it ever happened before. Yet even now the people who are looking on in astonishment do not understand. They think it is all very funny. Noah, they say, has decided to turn his ark into a zoo, seeing he couldn't get it to float.

But as the last of the animals passes through the door, Noah comes to the side of the ark and makes a final plea to the people to follow them in. "There is going to be a great flood!" he cries.

"The whole world is about to be destroyed. That is why the animals have come. They understand. Come! Come, before it is forever too late!"

But still no one responds. Again they laugh at him. "Go live with your animals," they sneer as they return to their homes and their sins.

Now God speaks to Noah again. "Come thou and all thy house into the ark," He says, "for thee have I seen righteous before me in this generation. . . . For yet seven days, and I will cause it to rain upon the earth forty days and forty nights; and every living substance that I have made will I destroy from off the face of the earth."

There is nothing more to be done. The people have had their chance. They have been given their warning. But they don't care. Blinded by sin, self-satisfied, and set in their evil ways, they don't even want to be saved. Their ears are deaf to God's message.

So Noah leaves them. The Bible says, "And Noah went in, and his sons, and his wife, and his sons' wives with him, into the ark, because of the waters of the flood. Of clean beasts, and of beasts that are not clean, and of fowls, and of every thing that creepeth upon the earth, there went in two and two unto Noah into the ark, the male and the female, as God had commanded Noah."

"And the Lord shut him in."

As the great door closes, silently and mysteriously, shut by an unseen hand, Noah catches one last glimpse of the beautiful world outside, the world he will never see again.

112

STORY 4

Heaven's Floodgates Open

INSIDE the ark Noah waits and wonders. For seven long days his faith is tested. Has he done right? Has he preached the truth? Will the Flood really happen as he predicted?

Outside some of the people begin to wonder too. The shut door bothers them. Perhaps they should have listened to Noah and gone in. Maybe the old man was right, after all. But since nothing happens, they soon get over their fears and smile again at the thought of Noah inside there with all those animals.

The days pass by. The last days of the world. Three, four, five, six.

Seven days later, morning dawns. But, instead of brilliant sunshine, black, angry clouds cover the sky. Lightning flashes. Thunder roars. Drops of water begin to fall. It is raining for the first time in the history of the world. Water from the sky! Just as Noah said would happen! The old preacher was right, after all.

8

Now there is a heavy downpour, increasing every minute. Water begins to pour off the roofs of houses and rush down the roadways. Streams fill up and overflow their banks. Low-lying land becomes swampy. Small lakes form everywhere.

Now there is water all over the place. Streets, basements, lower floors of houses, are all flooded. People begin to rush upstairs onto their roofs. Some look toward the ark and wish they had gone inside while the door was still open. Others leave their homes and hurry to higher ground. But the water follows them.

"It is the Flood!" they cry. "Noah's Flood is upon us!"

But worse is to come.

Look over there! What can that be? A wall of water rushing in from the sea. A tidal wave!

Now everybody runs for dear life. They climb trees and rush frantically up hillsides. But still the water rises higher and higher.

HEAVEN'S FLOODGATES OPEN

There is no escape, for "the same day were all the fountains of the great deep broken up, and the floodgates of heaven were opened."

Now some are trying to scramble up the steep sides of the ark. They batter frantically at the door. "Open!" they cry. "Open the door! Let us in! We are sorry for our sins!" But it is too late to be sorry now.

Swiftly the water rises, rises, rises. Houses are washed away. Forests disappear. Hills become islands, then vanish beneath the waves.

Panic-stricken groups of people, clinging desperately to the last high rocks, become smaller and smaller as first one, then another, loses his grip and plunges into the raging seas.

Higher and ever higher rises the water until finally "all the high hills" and even "the mountains" are covered.

Meanwhile, the wind-lashed tide has surged around the ark, beating on it, tugging at it, splashing over it.

The mighty ship rolls, heaves, lifts. It's off!

Yes! With its priceless cargo of life it is on its way from the old world to the new.

STORY 5

Strangest Voyage in History

BORNE up on the raging waters, the ark was swept forward by fierce tides and howling gales on the strangest voyage in history.

Only a vessel of the strongest construction and finest workmanship could have withstood the stresses and strains of those first few days and nights when, with awful earthquakes, "all the fountains of the great deep" were broken up and the floodgates of heaven" rained down their deadly deluge.

There was nowhere for the ark to go—no harbor anywhere —for "all the high hills, that were under the whole heaven, were covered." So it just drifted hither and yon, rolling and tossing this way and that as the terrific currents were "going and returning."

Rising to meet one giant comber, it would plunge down again into the trough of the waves, only to meet another towering whitecap rushing toward it. Again and again it must have been struck by huge walls of water that swept over it from stem

to stern. Floating trees and logs must have been a constant peril. That it didn't capsize and sink is a miracle.

Conditions inside were hard to endure—the violent movement, the lack of light and fresh air. Worst of all was the uncertainty, the endless wondering how it would all end.

Big as the ark was, Noah and his family were the only passengers. There was room for hundreds more, but nobody else chose to come aboard. And now all those who had refused to come were drowned. Everybody. Men and women, boys and girls. In all the wide world no trace of life was left. The old world had completely disappeared beneath billions of tons of water. "And all flesh died that moved upon the earth. . . . Both man, and cattle, and the creeping things, and the fowl of the heaven; and they were destroyed from the earth: and Noah only remained alive, and they that were with him in the ark."

How God must have watched over the ark through this whole fearful experience!

Did you ever stop to think how much it meant to Him? All His hopes and plans for the world depended on that little handful of people inside it. Only through them could His promises be fulfilled. Only through somebody in that storm-tossed ship could the Seed of the woman ever bruise the serpent's head.

How Satan must have tried to sink the ark in the height of the tempest! Could he have done so, he would have succeeded in defeating God's purpose. But the ark did not sink. Miraculously it rode out the storm.

"And God remembered Noah, and every living thing, and all the cattle that was with him in the ark: . . . and the rain from heaven was restrained. . . . And the ark rested . . . upon the mountains of Ararat."

Yet even after the ark had touched ground there was still no land to be seen—only water, water, everywhere.

118

STRANGEST VOYAGE IN HISTORY

The cessation of movement, the increasing stillness, the fact that there were no more big waves hitting the sides, told Noah that the worst of the Flood was over and that the water must be going down.

"And the waters decreased continually until the tenth month: in the tenth month, on the first day of the month, were the tops of the mountains seen."

What a day was that! And what a shout must have gone up from all eight of them at the welcome sight! "Land! Land!" they must have cried, with the joy of those who have been long at sea.

Now Noah "opened the window of the ark," and let out two birds, first a raven, then a dove. The raven flew happily "to and fro," but the dove returned, and Noah decided to wait a week and see how far the water would go down by then.

At the end of the week he let the dove go again. This time it came back with an olive leaf in its beak. All were cheered at this, for it showed that not only were the waters still going down, but that there were still at least a few trees standing.

Noah waited another week, and then sent the dove out once more. This time it did not return, and Noah felt sure there must now be much land free of water. So he "removed the covering of the ark, and looked, and, behold, the face of the ground was dry."

The rain had stopped, and the sun was breaking through the clouds. The Flood was over. And the strangest voyage in history had come to an end in the strangest way you could imagine, with the ark resting on a mountaintop in Asia Minor.

STORY 6

Beginning Again

NOW CAME the great moment for which all in the ark had been waiting so long—the opening of the great door that God had closed.

No doubt Noah and his three sons tried to roll it back. At last it creaked open, as if moved by the same mighty hand that had closed it. How glad everybody must have been to step outside and breathe the sweet, fresh air again!

So thankful was Noah for the way God had saved him and his family from the Flood that the very first thing he did as he went ashore was to build an altar and offer in sacrifice upon it at least one of "every clean beast, and of every clean fowl."

And that was a real sacrifice just then when the only animals in the whole wide world were those he had brought with him in the ark.

God was so pleased that Noah had remembered to say Thank you for his deliverance that He said, "I will not again curse the ground any more. . . . While the earth remaineth, seedtime and harvest, and cold and heat, and summer and winter, and day and night shall not cease."

Now, at God's command, all the other birds and beasts were released. What a sight that must have been! What a whirring of wings as great eagles, storks, herons, and flamingos leaped into the air and flew out to freedom, with robins, sparrows, thrushes, and linnets fluttering and hopping along behind them! How the nightingales must have trilled, and the blackbirds have squawked, and the mockingbirds have sung everybody's song at once in that moment of glad liberation!

Lions and tigers, buffaloes and hippos, elephants and giraffes, sheep and goats, dogs and cats, hurried through the great doorway, jostling one another as they bounded down the ramp in their eagerness to get out in the open again. And what a noise they must have made as each one sounded forth his joy, the lions roaring, the elephants trumpeting, the horses neighing, the oxen lowing, the donkeys braying, and all the little dogs barking their loudest!

Many of the animals disappeared at once, racing down the mountainside till they were out of sight. Others stayed around, liking human companionship, and Noah may well have wondered what he would do with so many if they continued to stay near the ark. But two by two, and group by group, they began to move away, wandering north, south, east, and west, seeking food and shelter. At last only some of the cows, sheep, goats, and, of course, the little dogs and cats, were left.

Meanwhile Noah and his family were looking around at the wild-looking place to which the ark had brought

them. It was a sad sight that met their gaze. Everywhere was wreckage and ruin caused by the raging waters. Great trees lay uprooted. Lovely hills had been swept clean of soil, leaving nothing but bare rock. Mountains had become scarred and jagged. Once-fruitful plains were deserts.

Not a single human dwelling was to be seen anywhere. Of all the beautiful homes they remembered, not a trace remained. All had been smashed to matchwood by the towering tidal waves that had swept over everything when the Flood began. It was enough to break their hearts.

As they stood there viewing the desolate scene, they felt the earth shake under them, for there must have been many a quake as the earth settled after the great eruptions when "all the fountains of the great deep" were "broken up." No doubt they felt afraid and lonely on that shuddering mountainside. Well may they have wondered what terrible thing was going to happen next.

Then of a sudden Noah looked upward, and there in the sky he saw something he had never seen before. As though trying to encircle the ruined earth with arms of love was a glorious, glowing arch of many colors.

Scarce daring to breathe, they all stood looking at it, struck dumb with amazement. What was it? What could it mean?

It was the first rainbow.

And as they watched in wonderment God drew near and said, "I do set my bow in the cloud, and it shall be for a token of a covenant between me and the earth. And it shall come to pass when I bring a cloud over the earth, that the bow shall be seen in the cloud: and I will remember my covenant, which is between me and you and every living creature of all flesh; and the waters shall no more become a flood to destroy all flesh.

"And the bow shall be in the cloud; and I will look upon it, that I may remember the everlasting covenant between God and every living creature of all flesh that is upon the earth."

It was God's way of saying, "I have not forgotten you. Nor shall I ever forget you, or My promises to you. When you see the rainbow and I see the rainbow, we will remember each other."

Only a God of love could have thought of speaking to His children in such a way at such a time. Having lost everything—money, home, all save life itself and what they had brought with them in the ark—these poor, homeless pilgrims surely needed a message of comfort and hope such as this.

But now, their hearts cheered, their courage renewed, they told themselves again that all would be well at last. How good to know that God was still with them, that God still loved them! And so, hand in hand with Him, they went forth through the shining arch above them to build a new world with Him.

STORY 7

The First Skyscraper

HOW LONG Noah and his family stayed on Mount Ararat nobody knows. It is quite likely that they made it their home for a long time, using the ark as a storehouse for the food and seed they had brought with them.

There was indeed nowhere else for them to live. Not a house or a building of any kind. So here they stayed while Shem, Ham, and Japheth went exploring in the nearby valleys looking for a good place to settle down and start farming again.

At last the day came when they decided to leave the ark and take all their belongings to their new home.

As they started down the mountain they must have looked back sadly many a time at the great ship that had meant so much to them all for so many years, until at last it was hidden from view in the mists that covered the peak. Whether they ever returned to it we do not know, or what became of it. Perhaps it was buried under the deep snow that later fell upon it, and finally rotted away.

124

THE FIRST SKYSCRAPER

The downward trek was difficult, for there was no road, of course, not even a trail of any kind. They had to clamber over jagged rocks, massive boulders, and fallen trees. In the hollows of the hills they came across large bodies of water and vast areas of swampy land. Every step of the way they saw fresh evidence of the awful destruction caused by the Flood. Everywhere there seemed to be some fresh mark of the curse that sin had brought upon the world.

But there was no time to be lost. They needed to build a new home, and quickly. For there was a baby coming. The Bible says that Arphaxad was born "two years after the flood." He was Shem's little boy, and Noah's grandson, and when he was born I am sure Noah was very proud of him. He is the first baby mentioned in the Bible as being born in the new world.

But he was not the only baby born in those pioneering days. Many other babies were born after him. Shem, Ham, and Japheth all had very large families. Soon the first home they built wasn't large enough to hold them all, and they began to spread out. As the children grew up and got married, they too went off and started homes of their own. Thus, slowly at first, then more and more rapidly, the earth began to be repopulated.

By the end of the first century after the Flood, Noah's family had grown into hundreds of families and lots and lots of children. There may well have been half a million people on the earth.

One of the big questions all these people talked about was where to live. Should they divide up and go away to some distant, unexplored part of the world, or should they stay near

home? Most of them decided they would rather keep together. Nobody wanted to go too far from great-grandfather Noah who, you will remember, lived for 350 years after the Flood.

Many times they must have talked about the beautiful world that Noah and his sons had known before the Flood, and how it was destroyed because of sin. What wonderful stories Noah could tell of those days!

Nobody doubted the Flood then. They were too close to it. And if anybody questioned whether the story of the ark was true, he could climb Mount Ararat and see for himself.

One day somebody raised the question, How do we know there will not be another flood that will drown us as our forefathers were drowned?

"But there's the rainbow," someone replied. "When we see that we are to remember God's promise that He will never again destroy the earth by a flood."

"But it isn't reasonable to trust our future and our children's future to rainbows," argued another. "We should do something about it and make ourselves safe in case another flood comes."

And so "they said one to another, Go to, let us make brick, and burn them throughly. And they had brick for stone, and slime had they for morter. And they said, Go to, let us build us a city and a tower, whose top may reach unto heaven; and let us make us a name, lest we be scattered abroad upon the face of the whole earth."

The idea caught on. Led by Nimrod, "the mighty hunter," everybody was soon helping to make bricks or carry them to the building site. Everybody, that is, except Noah and some others who remembered God's promises and trusted Him to keep them.

To build a tower to reach above the clouds was a very great task and must have taken a long time and lots of hard labor. But gradually it began to take shape. Week by week and month by month the world's first skyscraper rose above the Plain of Shinar.

As it grew higher and higher, with long lines of people patiently carrying the bricks up the steep ramps, everybody felt pleased. Now they could build a large city around this tower and have a safe place of refuge should another flood come upon them.

But God was not pleased. He does not like His word doubted, any more than you or I do.

The Bible says that "the Lord came down to see the city and the tower, which the children of men builded."

Of all the hundreds of busy builders not one realized that God was so near. But He was, right beside them. They thought they were getting along very nicely without Him, but they weren't, not really. It is never wise to forget God, for He sees and knows everything we do.

And what did God think of the tower the people were building? Not much. Indeed it must have seemed very small and paltry to Him who made the mountains, who raised up the mighty Himalayas of India, the lofty Alps of Switzerland, the high Andes of Chile and Peru, and the great Rockies of North America! What a pitiful little pile of earth it was, after all!

THE FIRST SKYSCRAPER

Yet it was dangerous. God saw that it would tend to hold the people in one place, whereas He wanted them to spread all over the earth. Then, too, if they all stayed together, not only would a great city grow up here, but an empire which, controlled by evil men, could thwart His gracious purpose for mankind.

Something had to be done, and God chose a novel way to upset the program. He mixed up the builders' speech. In other words, He caused some to talk one language and some another, so that they couldn't understand each other.

The effect was amazing. Just imagine what would happen at school some morning if every child in your class suddenly began talking a different language. How far would teacher get with the lesson? And what sort of game could you play at recess? Everything would be one terrible muddle, wouldn't it? Most likely school would be closed and everybody sent home.

And that's just what happened at the Tower of Babel. An overseer called for more bricks, and a man brought him mortar. Another called for mortar, and got a load of bricks. When a worker was told to bring a trowel, he brought a hammer; and when asked for a hammer, he brought a shovel, or just walked away not knowing what was being said to him.

Soon voices were raised in anger, and before long all were shouting at each other, and striking each other, until confusion reigned everywhere.

Nobody could understand what had happened, and nobody knew what to do about it. One by one people got disgusted and walked off the job. Work on the tower stopped.

9

← PAINTING BY HERBERT RUDEEN   ©   BY REVIEW AND HERALD

The higher they built, the prouder they were of their tower. But suddenly their language was confused, and everybody had to stop building. They scattered in all directions.

On their way home some of them maybe went shopping, but they couldn't buy anything, for the storekeepers couldn't understand what they wanted. Pretty soon the whole place was in an uproar.

Then one man said to his wife, "This is terrible. Let's pack up and leave. I can't stand this any longer." So he gathered his belongings and his family, and perhaps a few others who could understand what he said, and went away.

Soon another man did the same, and another, and another. Little groups began moving off in all directions, until at last no one was left to go on building the tower.

There must have been some very sad partings. Boys and girls who had played together tried to say good-by, and found they couldn't. Maybe they smiled and nodded and squeezed hands, but the words they tried to say sounded odd and ugly. Worse still, they couldn't plan to meet again.

It was hard, but God was thinking only of their good. And they all needed to learn the lesson that it never pays to forget Him or disbelieve His promises.

PART IV

Stories About Abraham, Isaac, and Lot
(GENESIS 12:1-24:67)

HARAN

MT ARARAT

NINEVEH

TOWER OF BABEL

UR OF THE CHALDEES

THE COUNTRY OF ABRAHAM
*When God called him out of Ur
to the land of Canaan*

SODOM

QUADE

STORY 1

God Finds a Boy

I T WAS just about a hundred years after the Flood that God scattered the people who were building the Tower of Babel. We know this because a baby happened to be born just then who was given the name of Peleg, meaning "division," "for in his days was the earth divided." It is easy to count back to Arphaxad—the boy born to Shem two years after the Flood—and so find the date.

And now the people were moving away from Babel. Some did not go very far. One group, led by Asshur, Noah's grandson, traveled north about 250 miles and founded the city of Nineveh. Another group went south and built a town called Ur. Still others wandered westward into Europe, and many traveled east into India, China, Siberia, and perhaps across the Bering Strait into North America.

Soon villages, towns, and cities were springing up all over the place. Industries were started, for people needed tools for building, farming, and cooking. Somebody discovered iron ore,

133

While Abraham was living in the heathen city of Ur, God called him to leave his father's home and go out to a land that God would show him. He obeyed without questioning.

and started the steel industry. Someone else found copper ore and how to smelt it. Others came upon gold, silver, and precious stones buried by the Flood; and soon goldsmiths and silversmiths were making beautiful ornaments, some of which can still be seen today in museums. Boatbuilders began making small craft to ply on the Euphrates, then larger and larger vessels to sail out into the unknown seas beyond the Persian Gulf.

Sad to say, as the people became more and more busy, they began to forget God, just like their fathers before the Flood. Some even made idols and worshiped them. This is hard to understand, for Noah and his sons were still alive. Noah lived 350 years after the Flood, and Shem 500. And one would think that the influence of these men who knew what God had done in years gone by would have kept the others true and faithful. But it didn't.

No doubt these older men kept on telling how God had destroyed the world because of sin, and how He had saved them in the ark, but by and by it became to many only an idle tale. Nobody wanted to listen.

As the years passed, wickedness increased, for when people forget God they begin to sin.

Three hundred years after the Flood conditions were almost as bad as before it.

Looking upon the scene, God must have been very sad. Perhaps He wondered whether it might not have been better if the ark had never been built and everybody had perished in the Deluge. But, of course, He could not have let this happen, for had He not promised Adam and Eve in the Garden of Eden that someday He would restore all they had lost when they disobeyed Him? Had He not said that the Seed of the woman would bruise the serpent's head? Therefore He could not let the Seed perish till the victory was won.

There was only one thing He could do. Before the world became totally wicked again, He must find somebody through whom He could keep alive the knowledge of His truth and His purpose. Somebody who would love Him and be loyal to Him always. Somebody who would stand for right, truth, and goodness in an evil world. Somebody who would bring up his children properly and see to it that they too kept His law.

Could someone like this be found? Anywhere? In Nineveh, perhaps, or Babylon?—for both these cities were quite large by now. Where among all the people was there a boy upon whom God could depend to do what He wanted done?

At last His all-seeing eye turned toward that far-off city of Ur, known later as Ur of the Chaldees. Here lived a man called Terah, who had three sons, Abram, Nahor, and Haran. The youngest of them—later known as Abraham—was a good lad and loved the Lord. Someone, perhaps his mother, had told him the story of creation and God's wonderful love for Adam and Eve in the beginning, and all the joy and glory that were theirs as they walked and talked with Him. He had learned how sin had spoiled everything and how God through Noah—his own great-great-great-great-great-great-great-great-grandfather —had tried in vain to save them.

As again and again he had listened to the old, old story, Abraham had come to love God and to decide that He would serve Him all his days.

It wasn't easy for him to come to this decision, for most of the people of Ur—including his own father—were already worshiping idols. There were idols even in his own home. So Abraham had to take his stand for God all by himself. And God loved him for doing so.

For God was watching him, just as He watches every boy and girl today. And when Abraham made his great decision I can imagine God said, "Here is the boy I have been looking for. A boy who will not fail Me. A boy to whom I can tell My secrets and with whom I can trust the future of My plan for the redemption of the world."

More years passed. Abraham's brother Haran died, leaving a little boy called Lot. Not having any children of his own, Abraham took special interest in this nephew.

Then one day, when Abraham was grown to manhood, his heart still set on following the Lord, he heard a voice speaking to him, and he knew at once it was the voice of God.

And God said, "Get thee out of thy country, and from thy kindred, and from thy father's house, unto a land that I will shew thee: and I will make of thee a great nation, and I will bless thee, and make thy name great; and thou shalt be a blessing: and I will bless them that bless thee, and curse him that curseth thee: and in thee shall all families of the earth be blessed."

Suddenly a glorious vision spread out before Abraham. He saw what God was planning for him in the days to come. He saw beyond the walls of Ur to the ends of the earth. He looked beyond the present to the end of time. He saw himself becoming a blessing to all mankind. But this meant leaving home and friends and his old familiar town.

Would he go, or would he stay? For a moment all the future hung upon his decision.

STORY 2

All Aboard for Canaan

WHAT did Abraham do? Did he say, "Maybe I'll go, and maybe I'll stay"? No. He did not hesitate a moment. He decided at once to do as God had told him. The Bible says, "So Abraham departed, as the Lord had spoken unto him."

What a lot those few words cover! All the packing up. All the arrangements for the journey. All the saying of good-bys to friends and relatives.

You can imagine what excitement there must have been in Ur when the news leaked out that Abraham was planning to leave. No doubt the neighbors came around to inquire why Terah's property was up for sale, only to discover that the old father was going along too.

Abraham explained how God had called him to go to a new country, but they couldn't understand why. And when he told them he didn't know the name of the place he was going to, they probably thought he was mad. Why should

138

anyone in his senses want to leave a fine, thriving town like Ur of the Chaldees to go to a place he knew nothing about?

But Abraham understood. He knew what he was doing. The God whom he had loved since boyhood had spoken to him, and that was enough.

Perhaps he wondered just what God meant by those words, "In thee shall all families of the earth be blessed," for the only families he knew were those around his home and a few others a short distance from Ur. He could have had no idea of the plan that was in God's mind for him to become the head of a long line of godly men through whom at last Jesus would come to fulfill the promise made to Adam in the Garden of Eden.

But though he could not see what God saw, he was willing to trust Him and to follow wherever He might lead. And that is a good example for all boys and girls today. When God says, "Arise and go," it is good to obey Him without question. For God plans only for our good, and we may be sure that at the end of the journey He will have a rich blessing awaiting us.

Well, at last everything was ready. All the household goods had been wrapped up in bundles and tied onto the backs of animals. Abraham had taken a final look around to see that nothing of any value was left behind. The servants guarding the flocks and herds were all ready for the word to move.

In those far-off days people did not travel by truck or train, but on foot. Everybody walked, or rode on camels or asses. And when there were cattle and sheep to be taken along, the pace

had to be kept down to that of the youngest calf or lamb. They couldn't hurry, as we do now. There was no "stepping on the gas" and speeding things up. They just had to journey slowly, covering only a very few miles a day. That is why it took Abraham such a long time to get from Ur to Canaan, a distance of only six hundred miles.

Picture the caravan as it was lined up for the journey. First perhaps were a few goats, followed by a flock of sheep, and a herd of cattle, with hired men to look after them and dogs to keep them from straying.

Probably these servants had their wives and children with them, and all their possessions, for when the head of a family moved, all his helpers went along too.

Then came Abraham and his wife, Sarah, and old father Terah, all probably riding on camels or donkeys and followed by more animals and servants.

Somewhere in the procession was Lot, Abraham's nephew, who seems to have become part of his uncle's family after his father died. He too owned cattle, and had servants to mind them, which made the caravan longer still.

ALL ABOARD FOR CANAAN

Who gave the word to start we are not told, but it was probably Abraham himself. He didn't say, of course, "All aboard for Canaan," but what he did say meant the same thing. As his word of command passed down the long line of waiting people and animals, the servants sprang into action. Dogs began to bark. Kneeling camels, loaded with heavy burdens, rose to their feet and loped forward. Cattle surged ahead, glad to be on the move again. The younger children toddled along holding their mothers' hands, and bigger boys and girls romped around enjoying the excitement.

And all this because one man had heard the voice of God and decided to obey Him!

Yes, Abraham was on his way to a great destiny. Dimly, far in the distant future, he had caught a glimpse of a beautiful city, "whose builder and maker is God." He was exchanging little Ur of the Chaldees for the New Jerusalem.

Ahead of him, he believed, was the Land of the Promise made to Adam and Eve—Eden, glorious Eden, someday to be given back to the children of men. And he was going toward it.

STORY 3

A Good Man's Footsteps

HOW FAR the caravan moved that first day we do not know, but probably it wasn't more than a few miles, with all the stops that had to be made for feeding the animals and the children, and looking after their many needs.

And so it was day after day. Just a few more miles, and a few more miles. What faith Abraham needed to keep the vision of the beautiful city bright and shining in his heart all that long, long time!

At last they came to a place called Haran. It may have been named after Lot's father, and perhaps some of his relatives lived there. In any case Abraham decided to stop awhile and give everybody a rest. There were many things that had to be done for so large a company. Then, too, old Father Terah wasn't feeling well. So they camped at Haran and stayed there until Terah died.

While at Haran the caravan grew larger and larger. Lots of calves, kids, lambs, and baby camels were born. More boys

142

and girls arrived to swell the families of the servants. So by the time Abraham was ready to leave, his moving problems had increased greatly.

Then a number of people living in and around Haran asked if they could go along too. They had heard Abraham tell of the great God of heaven, whom he loved and worshiped, and who had called him to leave Ur of the Chaldees and journey to a new and better land. As they had listened to his wonderful story and watched his godly life, they had decided to join him; and Abraham agreed to take them with him.

So we read that, when the caravan was about to move again —on Abraham's seventy-fifth birthday—"Abram took Sarai his wife, and Lot his brother's son, and all their substance that they had gathered, and the souls that they had gotten in Haran; and they went forth to go into the land of Canaan; and into the land of Canaan they came."

It would have been far easier and more comfortable to have stayed in Haran, where everybody had been so friendly; but this, Abraham knew, would not be doing the will of God. He must go on, ever seeking the Land of Promise.

Now the journey was slower than ever, with so many more people and cattle in the party. They made only a short distance each day. But it didn't really matter, for nobody was in a hurry. They took their time and enjoyed the trip.

As they moved southward the scenery became more and more beautiful. Now and then they passed small settlements of people, descendants of pioneers who had moved from Babel two centuries before. They found them to be distant cousins, being

143

children of Canaan, a son of Ham; hence the name, "the land of Canaan," for the country we now call Palestine.

Sad to say, most of these people had forgotten God and were worshiping idols, or bowing down to the sun or moon as though they were gods. They looked with astonishment at this caravan of people who carried no idols and whose kindly, noble-looking leader was forever talking of One who made heaven and earth, and who wanted everybody to love and serve Him.

"And Abram passed through the land unto the place of Sichem, unto the plain of Moreh. And the Canaanite was then in the land. And the Lord appeared unto Abram, and said, Unto thy seed will I give this land: and there builded he an altar unto the Lord, who appeared unto him."

Many months had passed since he had set forth from Ur, and you can imagine how glad Abraham was to hear God's voice again. Now and then during all the long journey and the many delays he may well have wondered whether he was on the right way, and doing what God really wanted him to do. But now he knew. How happy he was that God was pleased with him!

In his joy he built an altar and offered a sacrifice, while he, Sarah, and Lot, and all the servants knelt in worship.

As the smoke of the sacrifice rose high in the air some of the Canaanites saw it and wondered what was happening. As they came to find out, and saw Abraham and all his company on their knees before God, their hearts were touched. They remembered what their fathers had told them of the great Cre-

10

← PAINTING BY RUSSELL HARLAN Ⓒ BY REVIEW AND HERALD

The first thing Abraham did wherever he pitched camp was to build an altar. Then he and his household would reverently worship God while the heathen looked on in wonder.

ator, and some decided that they too would like to worship Him as Abraham did, instead of bowing down to idols.

Wherever the great caravan paused Abraham built an altar, until the land was dotted with them, each a silent witness to his faith. When, years later, strangers found one of them and asked what it was, and who had built it, there was always somebody to say, "This is one of the altars of Abraham, servant of the God of heaven."

These altars marked the footsteps of a good man, a man of God, who was seeking to do right and witness for his Maker. We should do as he did.

As we move from place to place through life we should try to leave behind us memorials to our faith. Long after we have gone from one classroom to another, or from one school to another, or from one city to another, people should be able to remember us as children of God, who always stood for right and truth and fair play.

Not that we shall be a perfect example all the time. Even Abraham, while he was building his altars, made one big mistake. And the Bible tells us about it, so that we won't be discouraged if we should slip sometime.

"Going on still toward the south," Abraham led his caravan all the way to Egypt. And there he tried to deceive Pharaoh. Because Sarah was so very beautiful he was afraid the king would kill him and take Sarah for himself. So he said that she was his sister. In a way this was true, but how much better it would have been if from the start he had said she was his wife!

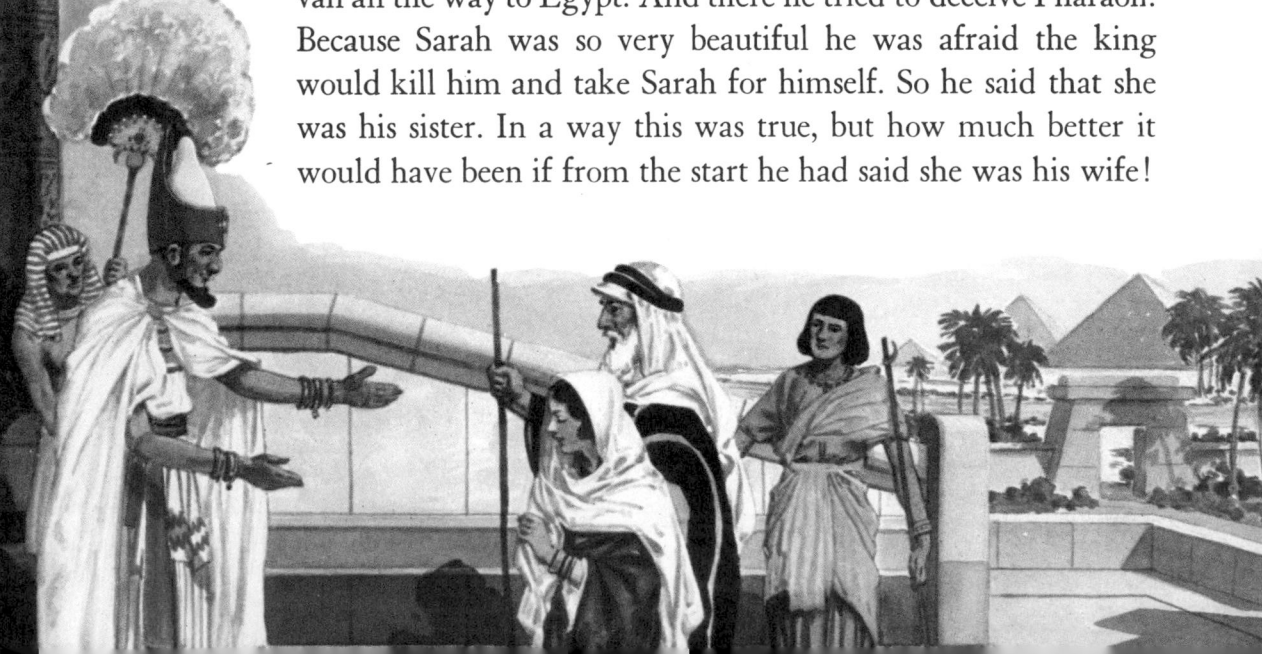

Pharaoh at first treated him royally and gave him many presents. But at last, as always, the truth came out. Then Pharaoh was angry, as he had reason to be, and Abraham was very much ashamed.

"And Pharaoh commanded his men concerning him: and they sent him away, and his wife, and all that he had."

In disgrace the caravan turned northward again. But though Abraham was heartsick at his failure, he knew where to go. "And he went on his journeys from the south even to Bethel, unto the place where his tent had been at the beginning, between Bethel and Hai; unto the place of the altar, which he had made there at the first: and there Abram called on the name of the Lord."

He had much to say to God. Oh, how he regretted that he had spoiled the best opportunity of his life to witness for Him— in Pharaoh's court! But God forgave him, and all was well again.

It is a good thing, when we make a mistake, to go back to some "altar" we built in "the beginning"—to some place where we met God before—and there pour out our hearts to Him in humble repentance. For He will hear us and forgive us, and we shall go on our way again, knowing He loves us still.

STORY 4

Choosing the Best

THE JOURNEY out of Egypt was not a happy one. True, Abraham had become "very rich in cattle, in silver, and in gold." So had Lot, who now had many "flocks, and herds, and tents." But there was a different spirit in the caravan. The servants were quarrelsome. When they camped at night there were angry words and blows.

The Bible says, "There was a strife between the herdmen of Abram's cattle and the herdmen of Lot's cattle."

One reason for the trouble was that there was not enough grass to feed so many animals. Quite likely too there were not enough wells at which to water them. "And the land was not able to bear them, that they might dwell together: for their substance was great, so that they could not dwell together."

Something had to be done. One couldn't journey to the Land of Promise with strife in the camp.

Now again we see the real greatness of Abraham. Calling Lot to him he said, so kindly and gently, "Let there be no strife,

149

The servants of Abraham and Lot quarreled over the division of the land, but Abraham was a man of peace, and he settled the trouble by allowing Lot to choose the best of the land.

I pray thee, between me and thee, and between my herdmen and thy herdmen; for we be brethren. Is not the whole land before thee? separate thyself, I pray thee, from me: if thou wilt take the left hand, then I will go to the right; or if thou depart to the right hand, then I will go to the left."

How generous of him! It surely was. Being in charge of the caravan, he could well have chosen the best for himself. But he didn't. Instead he gave his nephew the chance to choose. What an example to us!

Lot didn't deserve such kindness. After all that Abraham had done for him he should have said, "Dear uncle, you choose first, and I'll gladly take what is left." But he didn't.

Instead, "Lot lifted up his eyes, and beheld all the plain of Jordan, that it was well watered every where, . . . even as the garden of the Lord. . . . Then Lot chose him all the plain of Jordan; and Lot journeyed east: and they separated themselves the one from the other. Abram dwelled in the land of Canaan, and Lot dwelled in the cities of the plain, and pitched his tent toward Sodom."

Looking down from the mountainside upon the beautiful valley below, green and lovely in the morning sunshine, with the silver thread of the river Jordan running through the midst of it, Lot said to himself, "What a wonderful place to live! What fine pasture for my cattle! How rich I shall become down there!"

Perhaps, too, as he saw the valley dotted with little villages and the city of Sodom in the distance, he thought how nice it would be to settle down and be comfortable, instead of roaming

150

around the country with Abraham. What a good time he could have in Sodom, with its fine markets and many places of amusement!

He knew very well that Sodom was a wicked city, for everybody was talking about what was going on there, but he felt that it would be all right for *him* to live there. Nothing would happen to *him*. It might be dangerous for others, but he would be all right. Anyway, he would take the risk.

So Lot made his choice. He chose the plain of Jordan with its fine grazing land, its plentiful water, and its cities. And he "pitched his tent toward Sodom."

It was the worst thing he could have done, the biggest mistake of his life.

Unbeknown to him, that beautiful valley was soon to be a battlefield. The people living in those pretty little villages were soon to be taken captive by invading armies. But as for Sodom, that big, tempting city was about to be utterly destroyed by fire.

It never pays to be selfish. Sometimes a person who grabs the best for himself may seem to profit for a while. But in the long run he is bound to lose. We should pray for the grace and the greatness of Abraham, who gave first choice to somebody else.

STORY 5

Not a Thread or a Shoestring

I T WOULD seem as though Abraham was just a little bit discouraged as he saw Lot driving his flocks and herds downhill toward the Jordan valley, having chosen all the best land for himself. For just then God said to him, "Lift up now thine eyes, and look from the place where thou art northward, and southward, and eastward, and westward: for all the land which thou seest, to thee will I give it, and to thy seed for ever. . . . Arise, walk through the land in the length of it and in the breadth of it; for I will give it unto thee."

It was as though God said, "Cheer up! You don't need to mind that Lot chose as he did. All this land shall be yours, Lot's land too and all the rest—all the whole wide world."

At this Abraham was comforted and "removed his tent, and came and dwelt in the plain of Mamre, which is in Hebron, and built there an altar unto the Lord."

He had not been there very long, however, before he learned that Lot was in trouble, plenty of trouble. War had broken out when four kings, or rulers, of Mesopotamia had banded together to attack the kings of five cities around the Dead Sea, including the kings of Sodom and Gomorrah. It was "four kings with five," the Bible says, and the five lost.

The victors took everything they could carry away from Sodom and Gomorrah and "went their way."

"And they took Lot, Abram's brother's son, who dwelt in Sodom, and his goods, and departed. And there came one that had escaped, and told Abram the Hebrew."

What did Abraham do? Did he say, "Serves him right. He asked for it"? No. Instead, without a moment's hesitation "he armed his trained servants, born in his own house, three hundred and eighteen, and pursued them unto Dan."

We must remember that there were no policemen in those days. Abraham could not telephone the sheriff's office and ask for help. If Lot was to be rescued, Abraham and his servants would have to do it.

Knowing that his little band was greatly outnumbered, Abraham attacked at night, and his ruse was successful. He chased the enemy almost all the way to Damascus and rescued not only Lot and his family but all his goods, also all the spoil which the four kings had taken from Sodom and Gomorrah.

News of the victory spread quickly, and as Abraham returned with "Lot, and his goods, and the women also, and the people," he was the hero of the day. The king of Sodom came to meet him, feeling very grateful, as you can imagine. So did Melchizedek, king of Salem, who "brought forth bread and wine" in honor of the occasion.

NOT A THREAD OR A SHOESTRING

This Melchizedek, the Bible says, was not only a king but also "the priest of the most high God." When he saw Abraham he said, "Blessed be Abram of the most high God, possessor of heaven and earth: and blessed be the most high God, which hath delivered thine enemies into thy hand."

At this Abraham "gave him tithes of all," which means he took one tenth of all the goods he had recovered and gave it as a thank offering to this man of God. The rest he prepared to return to the king of Sodom.

Generously the king of Sodom said, "Give me the persons, and take the goods to thyself," but Abraham would have none of it. And here again we catch a glimpse of his greatness.

"I have lift up mine hand unto the Lord, the most high God, the possessor of heaven and earth," he said, "that I will not take from a thread even to a shoelatchet, and that I will not take any thing that is thine, lest thou shouldest say, I have made Abram rich: save only that which the young men have eaten, and the portion of the men which went with me."

Abraham had learned his lesson. He would not let the king of Sodom say, as Pharaoh had done, that he had made Abram rich. Never again would he accept favors from any earthly ruler. How could he oppose the wickedness of Sodom if he accepted money from its king? From now on his motto was, "Not a Thread or a Shoelatchet" from any source such as this.

And that's a grand principle for every boy and girl to follow. Never accept a gift that might tie your hands or silence your voice in your witness for right and truth. Never take a bribe of any kind, not even a thread or a shoestring.

155

Abraham was a very rich man and paid tithes of all his goods to Melchizedek, "the priest of the most high God." Melchizedek then blessed Abraham for his faithfulness and generosity.

STORY 6

Children Like the Stars

AS YEAR after year went by, Abraham began to wonder just what God had in mind for him. He had left Ur of the Chaldees as he had been told. Now he was in the land of Canaan, had been for a long time. Now what next?

He remembered how God had said to him, "I will make thy seed as the dust of the earth: so that if a man can number the dust of the earth, then shall thy seed also be numbered."

What did God mean by children like the dust, when still he had no child? True, he had lots of servants, and they had many children. He had thousands of animals, and they kept increasing every few months. He was getting richer and richer in gold and goods. But was this what God meant?

One day God said to him, "Fear not, Abram: I am thy shield, and thy exceeding great reward."

It was a most beautiful promise, but it did not answer the questions that had been growing in his mind.

"Lord God," he said, "what wilt thou give me, seeing I go

childless, and the steward of my house is this Eliezer of Damascus?"

By this Abraham meant that, seeing he had no son of his own, all his property would go at his death to his head servant, or overseer. It showed how low he was feeling at the moment.

God's answer sounded almost indignant.

"This shall not be thine heir!" Not Eliezer. Not this man from Damascus.

"Then who?" asked Abraham.

"Your own child," said God.

It was night, and God led him out into the darkness and said, "Look now toward heaven, and tell the stars, if thou be able to number them: . . . So shall thy seed be."

Abraham looked. And there above him he saw all the myriad twinkling pinpoints in the sky, each one a flaming sun in the far distances of God's infinite universe. Perhaps he started to count them, then realized he could never do it. Not if he counted all night. Not if he counted for the rest of his life.

Children like the stars! Thousands upon thousands of children! How could it be? How could he ever have that many children when he still had no child of his own? It seemed impossible.

Even so "he believed in the Lord," and the Lord "counted it to him for righteousness."

Then God said, "I am the Lord that brought thee out of Ur of the Chaldees, to give thee this land to inherit it."

"How shall I know?" asked Abraham, longing for some stronger evidence that this would really happen.

Then it was that God gave him a sign to put his old heart at rest. He was told to take a heifer, a she-goat, a ram, a dove, and a pigeon, and divide them. Having done so, he fell into a deep sleep. "And, lo, an horror of great darkness fell upon him."

Presently he heard the voice of God telling him about things to happen in the future: how he would surely have children, and no matter what trials they might pass through, God would watch over them always and at last fulfill every promise He had made concerning them.

"And it came to pass, that, when the sun went down, and it was dark, behold a smoking furnace, and a burning lamp that passed between those pieces."

Great darkness—then a light.

And what was this light?

A smoking furnace? A burning lamp? Oh, wonder of wonders, could this symbol of the presence of God be also the symbol of a star? Could it be that God was trying to tell his faithful servant that, while at last his children should be numberless as the stars of heaven, one of them was even now very close to him, coming sooner than he dreamed?

STORY 7

Sarah Laughs Too Soon

ABRAHAM was now so sure that somehow or other he must have a son that he talked the matter over again with his wife, Sarah. As a result they agreed that he should marry Hagar, Sarah's maid, an Egyptian woman.

In doing this Abraham made his second big mistake. He should have waited a little longer for God to work. Yes, I know he had waited a long, long time, but God was testing his faith for a purpose. He was to become known as the father of the faithful, and God wanted him to be a perfect example to all who should come after him.

And now this! It was too bad. Hagar bore him a son, but that didn't help matters at all. God had no intention of letting this boy, Ishmael, be Abraham's heir. He agreed to bless him because he belonged to Abraham, but the Promised Seed, He said, would never come through him.

Another thirteen years went by. Abraham was now ninety-nine years of age. Nearly a hundred, and still no son by Sarah.

159

Surely it was hopeless now. Perhaps he had been mistaken after all about that star that seemed to be coming straight toward him. Perhaps God had meant something quite different.

How often he must have been tempted to doubt! Then one day God spoke to him again, saying, "A father of many nations have I made thee. And I will make thee exceeding fruitful."

Then God mentioned Sarah, poor, old, wrinkled Sarah, now over ninety.

"I will bless her," He said, "and give thee a son also of her: yea, I will bless her, and she shall be a mother of nations; kings of people shall be of her."

This was almost too much for Abraham. His faith had held up till now but, well—Sarah!

"Then Abraham fell upon his face, and laughed, and said in his heart, Shall a child be born unto him that is an hundred years old? and shall Sarah, that is ninety years old, bear?"

Yes, he laughed. And when he told Sarah she laughed also. Maybe God smiled too, knowing what a surprise He was going to give them both very soon.

And the surprise came, all right, just when least expected, and when it seemed altogether impossible.

"And the Lord visited Sarah as he had said," and she "bare Abraham a son in his old age, at the set time of which God had spoken to him."

Thus was Isaac born, the son of promise—indeed, of many promises—and great was the rejoicing in the camp of Abraham. We can hardly imagine how happy those two dear old people must have been after waiting so long. No wonder we read that "Abraham made a great feast the same day that Isaac was weaned." He had something to celebrate in a big way.

And I like to think that, in the midst of the feasting and the rejoicing, when all the people from far and near were crowding around to offer their congratulations, Abraham lifted up his heart to God and said, "Thank you, dear God; thank you for my baby son. This is our first speck of dust, our first tiny star."

And Sarah? I can hear her saying, as she held her baby tight in her arms, "You were right, dear Lord, you were right after all; there is nothing too hard for you."

STORY 8

Fire Falls From Heaven

IT WAS about this time that God told Abraham what He was planning to do with Sodom and Gomorrah.

Year after year these two cities had become more and more wicked, until at last God decided that both must be destroyed. They were so bad they were a danger to all the people around.

Lot should have taken his children away from all this evil, but he had not done so. Now he could not leave. His wife liked living in Sodom, and his daughters had married worldly young men who had grown up in the city. He was in a hard place.

As the day of destruction drew near the Lord said, "Shall I hide from Abraham that thing which I do?" No, He answered, I shall tell him, for "I know him, that he will command his children and his household after him."

That was a wonderful thing for God to say about a man—"*I know him.*" God felt He could trust Abraham, not only today, but tomorrow and always. He knew Abraham was not only trying to live right himself but could be counted on to bring up his children in the way of God's commandments. So God felt free to let him into the secret of the coming punishment of Sodom and Gomorrah.

When Abraham heard the news his first thought was for his nephew, Lot. Seeking to save him, he said to the Lord, "You won't destroy the righteous with the wicked, will you? Maybe there are fifty good people there. If there are, surely you won't punish them with the rest? Shall not the Judge of all the earth do right?"

God was pleased that Abraham was moved with compassion for those people in Sodom who might not deserve to be punished, and He said, "If I find in Sodom fifty righteous within the city, then I will spare all the place for their sakes."

Abraham thought for a moment. Perhaps there might not be as many as fifty good people in the city. Then what? So he brought the number down to forty-five. And God said, "If I find there forty and five, I will not destroy it."

"Well," said Abraham, "how about forty?"

"I will not do it for forty's sake," God said.

Abraham's courage rose. Perhaps God would spare the city if thirty good people could be found there.

"I will not do it," God answered, "if I find thirty there."

Again Abraham lowered the number. This time to twenty. And God agreed not to destroy Sodom if twenty good people were there.

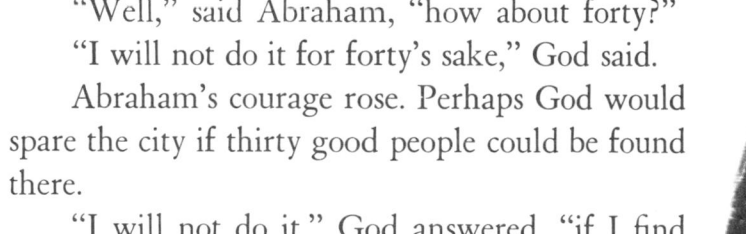

"How about ten?" And God said, "I will not destroy it for ten's sake."

Ten righteous people could have saved Sodom. But there were not ten there, so very wicked had that city become.

A little while after this two angels, in the form of men, arrived in Sodom. They went straight to Lot's house to warn him of what was about to happen. Barely were they inside, however, when a crowd of evil-minded men gathered outside the door and started a riot. They had seen two strangers enter and were determined to attack them. Lot went out to plead with them, and they turned on him. Only the prompt help of the angels, who blinded the rioters, saved his life.

Dragging Lot indoors, the angels told him of their mission and what was going to happen to Sodom in the morning.

It was hard for Lot to realize that this was Sodom's last night, and that he, his children, and all he owned would be burned up unless he acted at once.

The angels urged him to think quickly.

"Hast thou here any besides?" they said. "Son in law, and thy sons, and thy daughters, and whatsoever thou hast in the city, bring them out of this place: for we will destroy this place, because the cry of them is waxen great before the face of the Lord; and the Lord hath sent us to destroy it."

At last Lot was convinced that something terrible was really going to happen, and he went out "and spake unto his sons in law, which married his daughters, and said, Up, get you out of this place; for the Lord will destroy this city. But he seemed as one that mocked unto his sons in law."

The young men thought that Lot must be drunk or out of his mind. Certainly they did not believe him. There was no sign of coming trouble anywhere. And who was this God who said He would burn the place up? Absurd! No one was going to burn Sodom.

Lot himself began to doubt. As morning dawned, and fire was about to fall from heaven, he still wanted to stay in the city.

"And while he lingered, the men laid hold upon his hand, and upon the hand of his wife, and upon the hand of his two daughters; the Lord being merciful unto him: and they brought him forth, and set him without the city."

"Escape for thy life!" they urged. "Look not behind thee, neither stay thou in all the plain; escape to the mountain, lest thou be consumed."

No doubt the angels warned the little group not to look back because of the blinding flash of light and the powerful shock wave that would occur as the fire from heaven hit the city.

"Then the Lord rained upon Sodom and upon Gomorrah brimstone and fire from the Lord out of heaven; and he overthrew those cities, and all the plain, and all the inhabitants of the cities, and that which grew upon the ground."

From far up in the mountains Abraham saw the awful glow in the sky and knew what had happened. "And he looked toward Sodom and Gomorrah, and toward all the land of the plain, and beheld, and, lo, the smoke of the country went up as the smoke of a furnace."

Perhaps he wondered whether anybody could have been saved from this inferno. There must, he thought, have been fewer than ten righteous people there, or this would never have happened. But how many? He could not tell, but the answer was three—Lot and two of his daughters. For Lot's wife, her heart still in Sodom, had disobeyed the command not to look back, and had been instantly killed. She had become "a pillar of salt," the Bible says.

Now these three frightened souls are hurrying for dear life up the mountainside through a dense pall of hot, sulfurous smoke—the only people left alive in all that once-beautiful country.

Everybody else has been killed. Everything they once owned and loved has been destroyed—the cities, the trees, the lovely

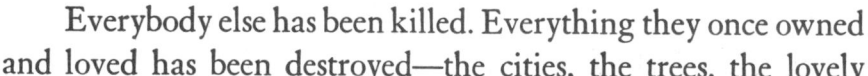

green pastureland. Everything that once had seemed so good to Lot and had led him selfishly to choose it for himself. Nothing is left save a great burned-over area. Even today, thousands of years later, the whole district is a wilderness, and the site of Sodom is covered by the Dead Sea.

So Lot, who once tried to grab the best, found himself at last with nothing. He had lost his home, his wife, his children and grandchildren, his barns and animals—all but the two daughters whom the angels had led to safety with him.

"And he dwelt in a cave, he and his two daughters."

That is the last we hear of Lot. What a sad end to a journey that began so happily and hopefully in Ur of the Chaldees! What lessons it has for us today! Surely it never pays to be selfish, and choose the best for ourselves. And how dangerous it is to play with evil, and pitch one's tent toward Sodom!

STORY 9

Love's Greatest Test

AS WE learned in Story Seven, Abraham was a hundred years old when his long-promised baby arrived. What a day was that! I can imagine that he and Sarah gazed upon the wee thing with such wonder and delight they could hardly believe their eyes. They called him Isaac.

Sarah was so happy she said, "God hath made me to laugh, so that all that hear will laugh with me."

When Isaac was a few days old Abraham had a big party and invited all his friends and neighbors to come and see the baby. How proud he was of it! And what a wonderful time he and Sarah must have had showing him off to everybody! I can almost hear Abraham saying, over and over again, "This is the baby God promised us when we left Ur of the Chaldees twenty-five years ago. This is our first little speck of dust, our first tiny star."

But everybody in the camp was not happy. Hagar knew that, now Isaac had come, her son Ishmael—now fourteen years

168

of age—would never stand a chance of being Abraham's heir. In her jealousy she poked fun at Sarah and her baby. So did Ishmael. At last Sarah became so angry she asked Abraham to get rid of them both.

Unwilling to do anything that might seem unkind, Abraham talked with God about the trouble, and God said that it would be better to let them go, but not to worry, for He would look after them.

Early next morning Abraham bade farewell to Hagar and Ishmael, giving them food and water for their journey. It must have been a sad parting, and I can imagine the old man's eyes were filled with tears as the boy and his mother walked away and finally disappeared in the distance.

Alas, the bottle of water was not sufficient, and when it was empty both Hagar and Ishmael nearly died of thirst. The boy collapsed in the heat of the desert, and Hagar burst into tears. But God kept His promise to watch over them.

"And the angel of God called to Hagar out of heaven, and said unto her, What aileth thee, Hagar? fear not; for God hath heard the voice of the lad where he is. . . . And God opened her eyes, and she saw a well of water; and she went, and filled the bottle with water, and gave the lad drink. And God was with the lad; and he grew, and dwelt in the wilderness, and became an archer."

Back in the camp, life revolved around the new baby. Everybody's eyes were upon him. Abraham and Sarah could think of nothing else. How they loved that child! Having waited for him so long, they could never do enough for him.

And God loved him too. For Isaac was an important link in the chain of His plan of salvation. Through him, and his children, the Seed of the woman, Jesus, would come at last to bruise the serpent's head.

And then, for a reason that must have been terribly hard for Abraham to understand, God asked him to offer Isaac as a sacrifice—to kill him like a lamb, or a kid, or a calf, and burn him on an altar!

It must have come as a crushing blow to the old man. Here was the boy just growing into sturdy young manhood, the joy of his parents' hearts, the pride of the whole camp, and now God said, "Take now thy son, thine only son Isaac, whom thou lovest, and get thee into the land of Moriah; and offer him there for a burnt offering upon one of the mountains which I will tell thee of."

Poor Abraham! Surely no greater test of faith and love ever came to any man. After waiting for years and years for this dear boy, after telling all his friends and servants that he was the miracle child that God had promised him, after loving him with all the intense devotion that an old man has for an only son, he was now asked to lay him on an altar and slay him!

"Why? Why? Why?" he must have asked, over and over again. Surely it must be all wrong. Surely he must not have heard God aright. Surely God would never ask anyone to do such a terrible thing.

But Abraham knew that God had spoken to him, and though he could not understand the command, he decided to obey it. In his heart he was sure that the One who had called

170

him out of Ur of the Chaldees and watched over him through all his journeyings, and finally fulfilled His promise to give him a son, would not ask him to make such a sacrifice without good reason.

So, willingly, but with a heavy heart, he "rose up early in the morning, and saddled his ass, and took two of his young men with him, and Isaac his son and clave the wood for the burnt offering, and rose up, and went unto the place of which God had told him."

All day long they traveled, and all the next day. Just Abraham and Isaac together, with the two servants following behind, wondering what it was all about.

What a sad journey that was! It must have been almost more than Abraham could bear. Every step of the way his heart became heavier and heavier, and I dare say he could hardly look at Isaac without wanting to cry.

What did they talk about? No one will ever know; but we can be sure that when they did speak to each other, it was with great tenderness: Isaac out of loving regard for his aged father, and Abraham because of what God expected him to do on the morrow.

"Then on the third day Abraham lifted up his eyes, and saw the place afar off. And Abraham said unto his young men, Abide ye here with the ass; and I and the lad will go yonder and worship, and come again to you."

"And come again to you." What hope was in these words! Yet how could it be? If he obeyed God and killed his son, how could both of them ever "come again"? Unless—could it be?—

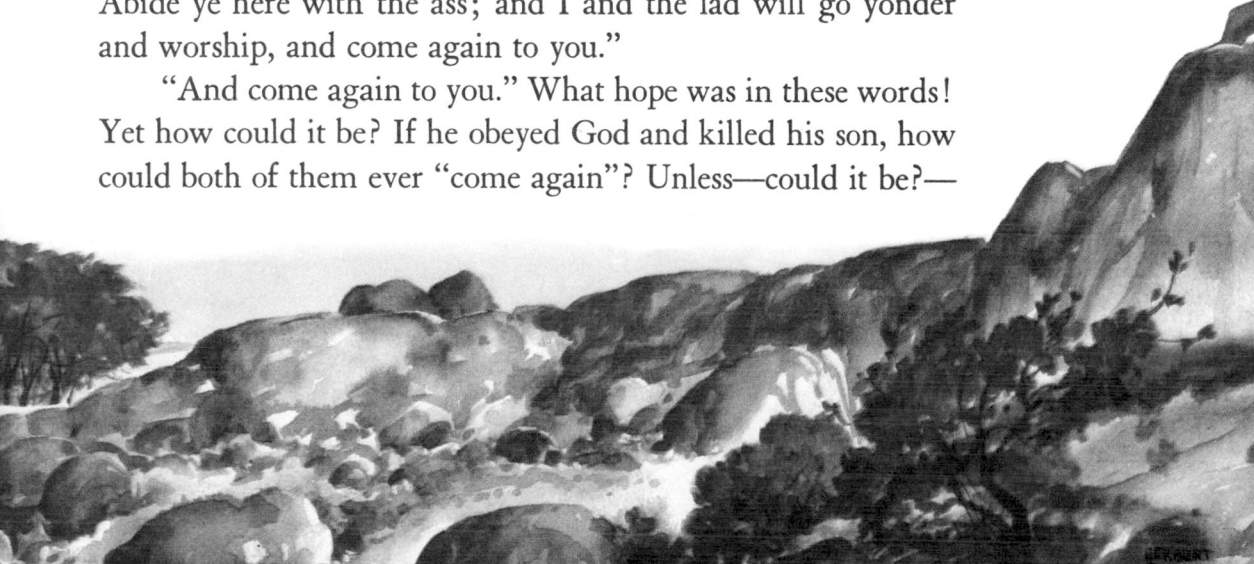

unless God planned to work a new and still greater miracle for him. It had never been done before, but, yes, God could do it! Had He not said that nothing was too hard for Him? Perhaps, then, it might even be that He would raise Isaac from the dead.

So we read in the book of Hebrews: "By faith Abraham, when he was tried, offered up Isaac: and he that had received the promises offered up his only begotten son, of whom it was said, That in Isaac shall thy seed be called: accounting that God was able to raise him up, even from the dead."

On the way up the mountainside Isaac began to wonder just what his father had in mind. Till now he had felt very proud and happy at being alone with him on this long journey to build a new altar to God; but now, as he looked over the things he was carrying, it suddenly dawned on him that something was missing. There was no animal for the sacrifice. They had traveled all this long way in vain. The most important item had been forgotten!

"My father," he said, "behold the fire and the wood: but where is the lamb for a burnt offering?"

So the moment Abraham had dreaded most had come! Isaac must be told the awful truth—but not yet, not till the last moment. So Abraham replied—and we can almost hear the tremor in his voice—"My son, God will provide himself a lamb for a burnt offering."

In saying this he said much more than he realized. His words were prophetic. For, long years in the future, God would do this very thing, not only for Abraham, but for everybody. He would provide a Lamb to die on Calvary—Jesus, "the Lamb

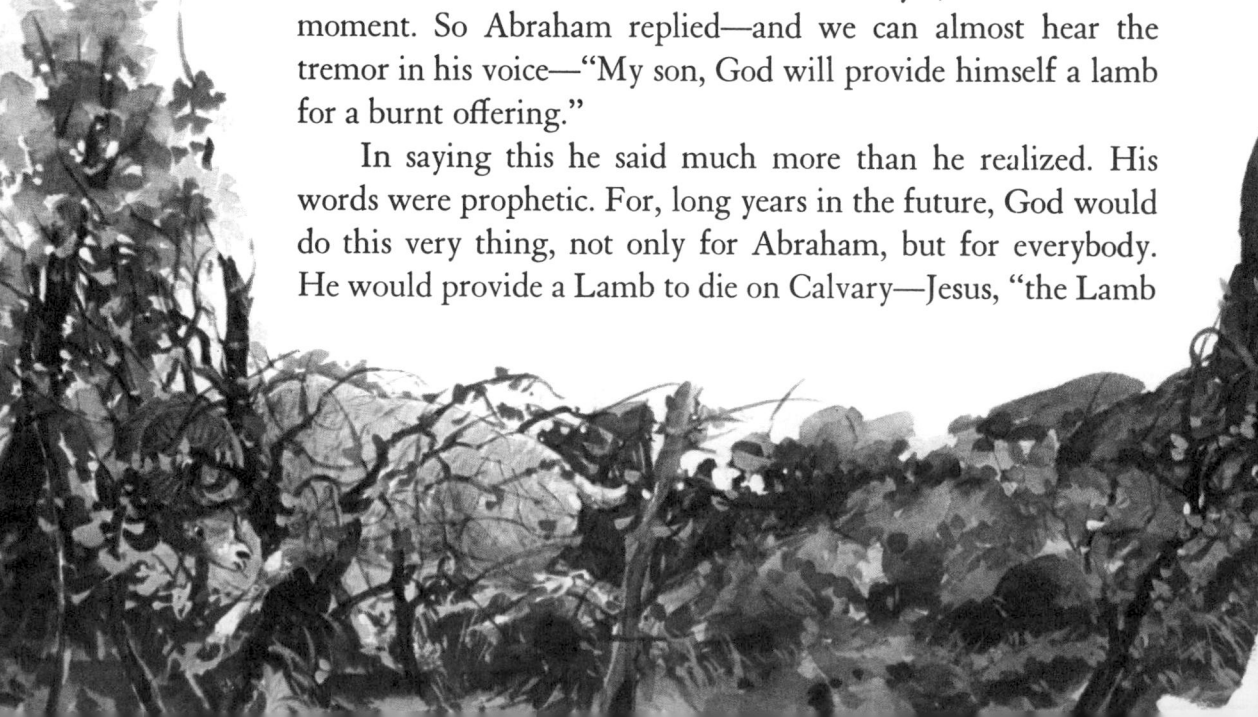

of God, which taketh away the sin of the world."

On they went together, with slow and weary steps, until at last they came to "the place which God had told him of; and Abraham built an altar there, and laid the wood in order."

Never had it taken him so long to prepare the wood on an altar, for he kept wondering and wondering whether God would do something to make the next step unnecessary. But nothing happened; and at last, turning to Isaac, he explained, as best he could, what God wanted him to do.

And here the beauty of Isaac's character is seen. He was young, strong, and vigorous. He could have resisted. He could have overpowered his old father and run for his life. But he didn't. When he understood that it was God's will that he should die, he yielded himself willingly, and Abraham "bound Isaac his son, and laid him on the altar upon the wood."

If ever heaven and earth were close together, it was at that moment. There was Abraham, standing by the altar, with tears running down his cheeks as he took one last look at the son he loved so dearly; and there was God right beside him, watching with infinite eagerness, wondering whether His faithful servant

could make so great a sacrifice without a question, without a word of complaint.

Would Abraham stand this awful test? Would he go through to the bitter end rather than disobey God?

"And Abraham stretched forth his hand, and took the knife to slay his son."

Isaac closed his eyes, awaiting the fatal cut. The knife flashed in the morning sunlight. But it never touched him. Suddenly the silence of that mountaintop was broken by the sound of a voice, loud, urgent, commanding, as though God Himself were anxious now.

"Abraham, Abraham: . . . Lay not thine hand upon the lad, neither do thou any thing unto him."

The voice came just in time. Another moment and all would have been over. Now the knife that might have killed the lad cut his bonds and set him free.

How the two of them, father and son, must have embraced each other in speechless joy at this amazing deliverance! And how God must have smiled upon them both for their love and devotion to Him!

Said the voice again, "Now I know that thou fearest God, seeing that thou hast .not withheld thy son, thine only son from me."

Then it was that Abraham saw a ram "caught in a thicket." Probably it had been there all the time, but both of them had been too worried to notice it. "And Abraham went and took the ram, and offered him up for a burnt offering in the stead of his son."

175

God honored Abraham's faith by restoring to him his son Isaac from the altar of sacrifice. They now lovingly embraced each other in gratitude to God for His wonderful goodness.

Then the voice came again, for God was still close by, happy in the knowledge that here was a man who loved Him with all his heart, who was willing to give up his dearest treasure at His command.

And the voice said: "By myself have I sworn, saith the Lord, for because thou hast done this thing, and hast not withheld thy son, thine only son: that in blessing I will bless thee, and in multiplying I will multiply thy seed as the stars of the heaven, and as the sand which is upon the sea shore; and thy seed shall possess the gate of his enemies; and in thy seed shall all the nations of the earth be blessed; because thou hast obeyed my voice."

Wonderful promise! In so saying God opened the whole treasury of heaven to his loyal and faithful servant. Everything God owns was made his forever.

And such is the blessing He offers to all who will love Him as did Abraham, who are willing to lay their best and choicest things upon the altar of sacrifice.

Dear boy, dear girl, are you ready to do just this? To lay yourself upon this altar? To devote your life to God and His service? Will you say to Him gladly and willingly—

> "Take my life and let it be
> Consecrated, Lord, to Thee"?

If so, then God will say to you, as He said to Abraham, "In blessing I will bless thee . . .; because thou hast obeyed my voice."

Then all your life will be different, radiantly happy and beautiful, as you walk with God toward the Land of Promise.

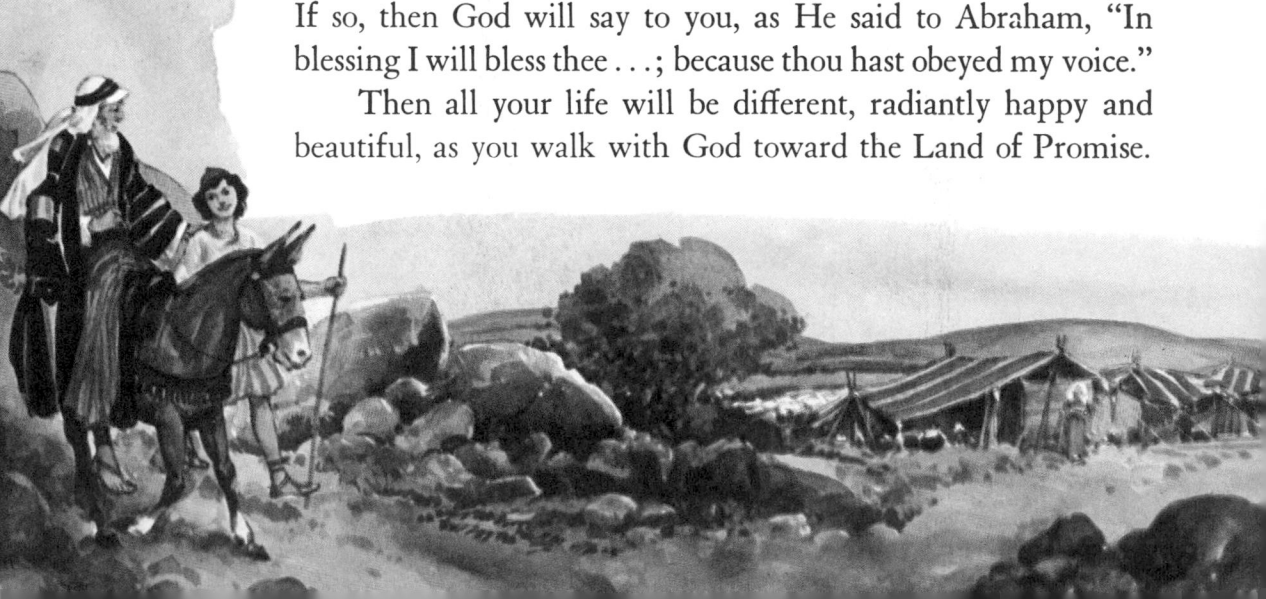

STORY 10

The Girl With a Kindly Heart

IT MUST have been a very happy journey for Abraham and Isaac back from Mount Moriah to Beersheba, where their camp was now situated. Father and son felt closer to each other than ever, and both were glad to know that God was pleased with them for what they had done.

On their arrival home they found interesting news awaiting them from Abraham's brother Nahor. There being no postal system in those days, the arrival of a messenger was an event of importance, and this one told how Nahor now had twelve children, two of them being called Huz and Buz, of all things! Another was called Bethuel, and he had a daughter Rebekah. This name didn't mean very much to Abraham at the moment. She was just another little grandniece. But someday she would become very important both to him and his precious Isaac.

Sarah was Abraham's big concern just now. She was 127 years old and failing fast. He knew she could not live much longer.

12

One sad day the dear old lady died, and her passing plunged all the camp in sorrow. You can imagine how lonely Abraham felt, and Isaac too, for, being an only son, his mother had meant much to him.

After Sarah was buried in the cave of Machpelah, Abraham began to worry about Isaac's future. The boy was old enough to get married, but to whom? The daughter of one of the servants wouldn't do—not in those days. And of course he mustn't marry a girl from one of the idol-worshiping families in Canaan, for she might lead him away from the true God.

What could be done about it? The matter was of great importance, for Isaac was sole heir to Abraham's great possessions, and the one through whom God's promise was to be fulfilled. And here he was with no wife and seemingly no way of finding one.

As Abraham thought about it he remembered his brother Nahor, the man with the twelve sons and many grandchildren. Perhaps one of his granddaughters might be suitable. Had not the messenger mentioned one of them? What was her name now? Rebekah. Yes. That was it. Rebekah. Well, at least he could find out.

So Abraham called Eliezer, his most trusted servant, and told him what he wanted him to do. "Thou shalt go unto my country," he said, "and to my kindred, and take a wife unto my son Isaac."

This meant a long journey, clear back to Haran in Mesopotamia, and Eliezer became worried.

"Suppose the girl won't come back with me?" he said.

178

THE GIRL WITH A KINDLY HEART

"Then what shall I do? Shall I take Isaac over there?"

"No!" said Abraham. "You must never do that. Beware thou that thou bring not my son thither again."

He was afraid that if Isaac were to return to the old home, he might forget all that Abraham had told him of God's wonderful leadings and His plans and promises for the future. Rather than have this happen, Abraham was willing to have Eliezer fail in his mission and return alone.

Of course, if Isaac had been like some modern young people, he would no doubt have insisted on going along with Eliezer and looking over all the girls himself, but in those days this would not have been proper. It could be, of course, that he told Eliezer quietly the kind of girl he would like to have for his wife.

The story of how the faithful old servant found the right girl—the girl with the kindly heart—is one of the sweetest in all the Bible.

Taking ten camels, Eliezer prepared quite a caravan; for besides having a long way to go, he also wanted to make a good impression on the young woman, should he be fortunate enough to find one.

As he journeyed on, day after day, he asked himself many times how he would know which was the right girl when he got to his destination. Suppose Nahor's granddaughters were all equally nice. Then what? And, dreadful thought, suppose he should bring back the wrong girl—someone whom Isaac would not like! Finding a wife for somebody else is no easy task.

Late one evening he came to Haran, the city where Nahor lived. Hot and tired, he made his way to the well outside the city gate and made his camels kneel down ready to be watered. Then he waited and watched, for it had occurred to him that this was the very time of day when the maidens of the city would be most likely to come to the well to get water for themselves and their animals. Should they do so, he would have a wonderful chance to look them over before they discovered who he was or why he had come.

But still he was bothered about how to choose the right one. If he should pick the prettiest, she might, at heart, be proud and selfish. If he should pick the best-dressed girl, he might find out, too late, that she was worldly and untrue to God.

Oh, dear, what was a poor man to do? How easy it would be to make a mistake!

And now the city gate is opening. Some maidens are coming out, their water pitchers on their shoulders. Could one of these be the girl for Isaac?

THE GIRL WITH A KINDLY HEART

Even as the maidens approach he sends up an urgent prayer to God for help. "O Lord God of my master Abraham," he whispers, "I pray thee, send me good speed this day, and shew kindness unto my master Abraham."

Then he suggests a simple test:

"Behold, I stand here by the well of water; and the daughters of the men of the city come out to draw water: and let it come to pass, that the damsel to whom I shall say, Let down thy pitcher, I pray thee, that I may drink; and she shall say, Drink, and I will give thy camels drink also: let the same be she that thou hast appointed for thy servant Isaac."

This test, you notice, was based, not on the prettiness of the girl's face, but on the kindliness of her heart; not on her clothes or her make-up, but on her thoughtfulness of others.

Carefully he watches the group of girls, wondering whether any one of them will do as he suggested. Some are plain and some good looking. Some are cheerful, and others glum. Some notice the stranger with the camels and smile at him; others turn their backs and ignore him.

Then one of them, fairer than all the rest, comes to the well and fills her pitcher with water.

Feeling impressed to speak to her, Eliezer says, "Let me, I pray thee, drink a little water of thy pitcher."

The girl answers, "Drink, my lord." And taking the pitcher from her shoulder, she offers him a drink.

"I will draw water for thy camels also," she says, "until they have done drinking."

Hurrying as fast as she can, the girl empties her pitcher into the trough and runs again to the well to draw water for all the camels.

How much water those ten camels drank, I don't know, but I am sure that it must have meant a lot of work for that girl to draw it from the well and carry it to the trough. But she does it happily and graciously.

Meanwhile Eliezer looks on with increasing admiration, feeling more and more sure that this is the girl whom he is seeking.

Then what a surprise is hers! For now Eliezer, opening one of his bags, takes out some beautiful gold and silver orna-

ments and gives them to her. I can almost hear her crying out in surprise, "For me? I didn't expect to be paid for helping you, sir, but, oh, they are so pretty!"

Eliezer smiles. "Whose daughter art thou?" he asks. "Tell me, I pray thee: is there room in thy father's house for us to lodge in?"

"My name is Rebekah," she says. "I'm the daughter of Bethuel. Surely we have both straw and provender enough, and room to lodge in."

So this is Rebekah! The very girl he has wanted to see so much. To think that she should have been the very one to water his camels!

Quite overcome with his good fortune, Eliezer falls on his knees and pours out his thanks to God. "Blessed be the Lord

183

God of my master Abraham," he says, "who hath not left destitute my master of his mercy and his truth: I being in the way, the Lord led me to the house of my master's brethren."

Seeing the stranger on his knees, praying to the God of heaven, Rebekah turns and runs toward her house.

The first person she meets is her brother Laban, who, just like a brother, at once spots the expensive jewelry she is carrying.

"Where did you get it?" he asks.

"A man gave it to me. At the well. Come and see him."

Then she tells all that has happened, and how the stranger has traveled all the way from Abraham's house, far off in the land of Canaan.

Now Laban hurries to the well himself to find out whether what his sister has told him is really true. Seeing Eliezer, all his doubts vanish, and he says, "Come in, thou blessed of the Lord; wherefore standest thou without? for I have prepared the house, and room for the camels."

Servants rush to bring food and drink, but Eliezer will eat nothing until he has told his story. First he tells about Abraham, how God has greatly prospered him; then, how his master sent him to find a wife for Isaac; next, of his prayer at the well; and last, how Rebekah's kindly deed made such a deep impression upon him.

As Rebekah listens a blush comes to her cheeks. Her heart pounds. This is too wonderful! To think that she may become

the wife of the only son of Abraham—the great Abraham of whose riches and goodness she has heard from her childhood!

As Eliezer finishes his story Bethuel and Laban are sure God has been leading in all that has happened. "The thing proceedeth from the Lord," they say. "Behold, Rebekah is before thee, take her, and go, and let her be thy master's son's wife, as the Lord hath spoken."

Then all eyes turn to Rebekah, for she must have something to say about this.

"Wilt thou go with this man?" they ask.

"I will go," she says.

And that is what she did. The very next morning Eliezer's caravan started back toward Canaan with Rebekah seated on one of the camels, still wondering how such great good fortune could have come to her so suddenly.

Maybe she never realized it, but how much depended on that one kindly deed she did for a stranger! How much blessing and happiness she would have missed if she had been cross and grumpy that evening! All the future—for herself, her children, and her children's children, yes, and her part in God's great plan of salvation—hung upon her conduct at that moment. We never can tell how great a blessing even a smile or a friendly word may bring to us.

Meanwhile somebody in Canaan was waiting anxiously for that caravan. Abraham, surely, but Isaac, poor lonely Isaac, most of all. It was never out of his thoughts. Day after day he prayed that God would help Eliezer bring back someone he could love.

Then one day, as Isaac went out to pray "in the field at the eventide: . . . he lifted up his eyes, and saw, and, behold, the camels were coming."

The camels! How he had waited for those camels!

He counted them. There were ten. He felt sure it must be Eliezer's caravan. He scanned it from end to end, searching for a maiden's face. He thought he saw one, and hurried forward.

Meanwhile—very strangely, of course—Rebekah was looking around too with keen and wondering eyes. As the caravan drew near the camp, she said to Eliezer, "What man is this that walketh in the field to meet us?" He told her, and—well, it was love at first sight. And when "the servant told Isaac all things that he had done," Isaac had no doubt whatever that this lovely girl was indeed God's choice for him.

Then he did a very beautiful thing. He took her "into his mother Sarah's tent," and there recounted to his bride-to-be all the sweet memories it brought back to him.

After that he "took Rebekah, and she became his wife; and he loved her: and Isaac was comforted after his mother's death."

STORY 11

The Boy With a Friendly Spirit

IF REBEKAH was the girl with a kindly heart, Isaac was the boy with a friendly spirit. He was always thinking of others, and how he might help them. Nothing ever seemed to upset him.

You remember how he behaved on Mount Moriah, when his father explained that God wanted him to be offered up as a sacrifice; then how deeply he mourned for his mother, and how happy he was when he saw Rebekah. In all these ways he revealed the sweet gentleness of his character.

As the years went by the same lovely quality shone out again and again in his life.

When Abraham died in his hundred and seventy-fifth year, what do you suppose Isaac did? He sent for Ishmael, whom Abraham had sent away from the camp long years before. Together they buried their father in the cave of Machpelah, where Sarah had been laid to rest.

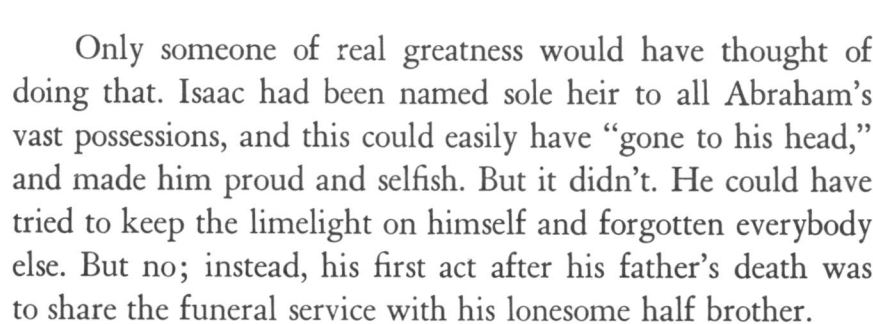

Only someone of real greatness would have thought of doing that. Isaac had been named sole heir to all Abraham's vast possessions, and this could easily have "gone to his head," and made him proud and selfish. But it didn't. He could have tried to keep the limelight on himself and forgotten everybody else. But no; instead, his first act after his father's death was to share the funeral service with his lonesome half brother.

Not long after this, Isaac heard that the Philistines were filling up the wells that his father had dug in various parts of the country. This news would have made most men very angry, for in those days, and in that sort of country, wells were of the greatest importance, being the only source of water for cattle.

No doubt while Abraham was alive the Philistines had envied him his large herds of cows and his many flocks of sheep and goats. And when they heard of his death they probably said to themselves, "Now is our chance to get some of his land for ourselves. Let's fill up his wells and drive his animals away. As for his heir, we don't need to worry about him. He isn't anything like as strong a man as his father."

But in Isaac they met a new kind of strength. He didn't attempt to fight them, as they thought he might. Instead he was just friendly to them. And that was something they didn't know what to do about.

THE BOY WITH A FRIENDLY SPIRIT

Coming one day to the valley of Gerar, Isaac's servants reported to their master that all the wells that Abraham had dug here had been filled in.

Instead of losing his temper, as others might have done, Isaac merely said, "All right, dig them again."

So his servants quietly went to work and reopened the wells. Hardly had they done so, however, when the local herdsmen crowded around and tried to start a fight. "That water is ours," they shouted.

"Very well," said Isaac. "Let's not fight about it." And he ordered his servants to move on a little way and dig another well.

Hardly had water been found in this new well, however, than the same people who had fussed over the first one came running up shouting, "That water is ours too!"

This must have been very hard for Isaac and his servants to take. Digging a well at any time is no easy job, and in that hot climate it must have been very hard work. And now to be told that the water they had labored to find didn't belong to them was enough to make most men want to fight back.

But not Isaac.

"You may have it," he said. "We'll go somewhere else and dig again."

And that is exactly what he did. The Bible says, "And he removed from thence, and digged another well; and for that they strove not: and he called the name of it Rehoboth [meaning, "room"]; and he said, For now the Lord hath made room for us, and we shall be fruitful in the land."

Truly the Lord did make room for Isaac, but He did it through the sweet and kindly spirit he showed to those who opposed him. They simply couldn't fight a man like that. So he won by just being patient and kind, and by so doing he left behind friends instead of enemies.

Just then, the very same night, the Lord appeared to him and said, "I am the God of Abraham thy father: fear not, for I am with thee, and will bless thee, and multiply thy seed for my servant Abraham's sake."

It was just as though God had said to him, "I am so pleased you acted the way you did over those wells. I love you for it. That is the spirit I want to see in all My children. Never fear to do right. Remember, I am always with you, and I am going to bless you as I promised your father Abraham."

This is something for us to remember when others are mean and rude to us. If we try to treat them kindly and tenderly, God will be as pleased with us as he was with Isaac, and the blessing He promised him will be ours also.

We know this is true because of what Jesus said one day, "Love your enemies, bless them that curse you, do good to them that hate you, and pray for them which despitefully use you, and persecute you; that ye may be the children of your Father which is in heaven."

If only every boy and girl were like Isaac and Rebekah, having a kindly heart and friendly spirit, what a happy place this world would be!

190